Me la Mander was born in Chingford, Essex, of a family with
mmon name rooted all over Britain. Perhaps as a
nce, she has always been addicted to social and family
Originally a journalist but now in commerce, the author
London University and has worked freelance for the
of Arms as well as lecturing on genealogy (the tracing
ly trees) for Waltham Forest Adult Education Service.
ber of the Society of Genealogists, she has written a
er of articles on family history.

Meda Mander

How to Trace Your Ancestors

MAYFLOWER
GRANADA PUBLISHING
London Toronto Sydney New York

Published by Granada Publishing Limited
in Mayflower Books 1977
Reprinted 1977

ISBN 0 583 12760 6

First published in Great Britain by
David & Charles (Publishers) Ltd 1976
as *Tracing Your Ancestors*
Copyright © Meda Mander 1976

Granada Publishing Limited
Frogmore, St Albans, Herts AL2 2NF
and
3 Upper James Street, London W1R 4BP
1221 Avenue of the Americas, New York, NY 10020, USA
117 York Street, Sydney, NSW 2000, Australia
100 Skyway Avenue, Toronto, Ontario, Canada M9W 3A6
Trio City, Coventry Street, Johannesburg 2001, South Africa
CML Centre, Queen & Wyndham, Auckland 1, New Zealand

Made and printed in Great Britain by
Hazell Watson & Viney Ltd
Aylesbury, Bucks
Set in Monotype Times Roman

CONTENTS

LIST OF ILLUSTRATIONS

PLATES

Family Bible (*from the author's collection*)
Birth certificate (*Crown copyright, reproduced by permission of Her Majesty's Stationery Office*)
Marriage certificate (*Crown copyright, reproduced by permission of Her Majesty's Stationery Office*)
Death certificate (*Crown copyright, reproduced by permission of Her Majesty's Stationery Office*)

IN TEXT

ABBREVIATIONS

BL   British Library
CRO   County or City Record Office
GRO   General Register Office
LRO   Land Registry Office
OS   Ordnance Survey
PCC   Prerogative Court of Canterbury
PCY   Prerogative Court of York
PRO   Public Record Office
RNR   Royal Naval Reserve

MONEY VALUES

1975	£1.00	1860	£11.62
1946	£4.59	1760	£18.98
1900	£14.35		

Pre-decimal shilling (1s)=5p

FOREWORD

My own interest in genealogy sprang simply from hilarious tales of her childhood recounted by a much-loved mother, and my hope is that those embarking on their personal search for family history may find in this book helpful but not too prosaic guidelines, covering the many innovations which have occurred in recent years.

Counties (unless stated otherwise) are as under the April 1974 alignment.

Very best thanks for co-operation are due to the Record Offices for Bedford, Berkshire, Buckingham, Cambridge (two), Cheshire, Clwyd, Cornwall, Cumbria (two), Derby, Devon, Dorset, Dyfed, East Sussex, Glamorgan, Gloucester, Greater London (Middlesex), Gwent, Gwynedd (three), Hampshire, Hereford & Worcester (two), Hertford, Isle of Wight, Kent, Kingston-upon-Hull, Lancashire, Leeds, Leicester, Lincoln, Norfolk, Northampton, Northumberland, Nottingham, Oxford, Salop, Somerset, Staffordshire, Suffolk, Surrey, Tyne & Wear, Warwick, West Sussex, Wiltshire and York, plus Powys County Council.

Particular thanks are offered to London's General Register Office and Public Record Office, HM Stationery Office, the County Record Offices of Durham, Essex and North Yorkshire, the Rector of Stockton-on-Tees, the Vicar of Northallerton and Bishopsgate Foundation.

This book exists due to the unfailing support of Jean Luxford and constant spurring of Jacqueline Lewzey, despite 'assistance' from a donkey-sized Alsatian puppy. It is offered as truly a labour of love, to light my own candle to the sun.

CHAPTER ONE

PLANTING THE SEED

They say that the art of good conversation is to get the other fellow to talk about himself, since nothing interests anyone more. Fascinating, then, to mould together all the pieces of personal heritage which go to make up oneself!

There is born in man a deep need, conscious or not, to belong. He is not by nature a 'loner'. This book sets out hopefully to help the beginner with his private detective work in following a story, full of fascination, revelation, and maybe celebration or consternation.

Ordinary modest individuals set out with a variety of goals. Two sisters with a sixteenth-century family parchment want to bridge the gap between it and themselves; a man wants to confirm his reputed descent from Charles II; a widow begins by wanting to trace her long-lost only sister; an illegitimate boy seeks a family background; another is curious because of his unusual surname; while others just become fascinated by anecdotes of parents' childhoods.

The art of tracing a family tree, genealogy, covers a much vaster hunting ground than may be apparent. The aim is not glory, fortune or the discovery of royal blood, but the fun and absorbing interest of tracing 'one's own', with perhaps a little notoriety thrown in for good measure and certainly a few surprises – some not particularly welcome. It can be an exhilarating hobby and is completely open-ended. As one family branch breaks off in the wind, some other part of the tree will always sprout another, for virtually every female who marries into a family links it to yet another surname.

It is highly unlikely you will trace your family back to Domesday, and in fact you will be lucky to reach the sixteenth century, but almost *any* distance is rewarding and interesting.

Properly, it is essential to prove authenticity by documents, helped by letters, newspapers, advertisements, inscriptions, heirlooms, etc. Usually documentary copies of records can be bought, and heirlooms are not necessarily anything more valuable than an inscribed watch or some such modest thing.

The whole interest in amateur genealogy is that you are following 'your own' and therefore yourself. It matters not where you start, but thereafter keep to one male line and don't go off at a tangent, trying to follow several surnames. If you get really stuck later or intrigued by a 'side' family, time enough then to change branches.

At least initially an unusual surname will probably help, but later can just as easily hinder. Later, too, there is sometimes great variation of spelling to be remembered when searching through alphabetical lists, which until around a hundred years ago were often not strictly alphabetical anyway and occasionally are not even now. A hundred years is not very long: allow an average of thirty years between male generations, i.e. roughly a hundred years from the birth of a man to that of his great-grandfather.

Be prepared to read a great many reference books and records. In your search you will practise at least a little deciphering of ancient writing. Learn something of social history to get the flavour of the times and throw a little light of probability on search problems, and perhaps get a smattering of heraldic knowledge.

You can do your tracing wholly by paying professionals, but this is expensive and without the thrill of personal discovery. You can, alternatively, use professionals only occasionally, when really stuck for a lead or physically unable to be in the right place. You can use students (especially those working on related subjects) willing to earn pin-money and accustomed to accuracy. But by far the most pleasurable way is to do the work yourself.

If you do employ professionals, the main source for England and Wales is the College of Arms, where the highly skilled heralds will undertake searches for whatever period or up to whatever cost is specified. This is expensive, not surprisingly, since £100 will not get you far today, and these gentlemen are top specialists in a most complex and scholarly field. However there is the comfort of knowing that no one is more reliable or thorough. Unless you contact the herald of your choice, your case will be dealt with automatically by the one dealing by rota that week with new inquiries. It is impossible to quote charges, but it is perhaps indicative that the 1976 fee for a personal coat of arms with crest was £480.

The College of Arms (or Heralds' College) is the official depository of all armorial records, handles all grants of arms and designs for them and holds the best collection of Welsh pedigrees, so if you believe you are entitled to bear heraldic arms then this is where inevitably you must inquire and where the heralds' word is law. However it does not follow, of course, that everyone will find themselves in this position.

In Scotland it is less expensive to employ the élite, that is Lord Lyon King of Arms and his heralds at New Register House, Edinburgh.

GETTING STARTED

Assuming that you are your own servant, you will need to know how to start climbing your tree.

The first rule is to work backwards. It is no good thinking if your name is Churchill that you *must* be related to Sir Winston. Surnames started in various ways anyway, and there were lots of hills with churches on top.

Note everything you know already by way of names, relationships, dates, locations, occupations, etc. It is essential to keep notes. I would suggest you start with two notebooks (loose-leaf preferably so that you can expand sections at will):

1 Alphabetically by family individuals
2 General notes.

For the first, have separate sheets for each individual. If there is more than one John, say, dub them 'grocer John Smith' or 'sailor John Smith' or 'Dr John Smith', or alternatively 'John Smith 1' and 'John Smith 2' – but use numbers *backwards* because you never know if you may finish with

John no. 3 or no. 15! Begin each sheet with basic details, including parents and children for cross-reference, and ideally use side-tabs. For the second, have separate sheets for each subject of interest, e.g. apprenticeships, books, overseas. You will also need an alphabetical file for correspondence.

Collect anything you can from the knowledge of parents, grandparents, other relatives. Even small details may be useful, for instance, if a dead ancestor pronounced some words like a Tynesider or Devonian, since this can help in knowing where to search. Individuals have been linked together before now by a predominant feature such as giant noses, piebald hair, long thin hands or even webbed toes. Undoubtedly someone sometime will mention some outlandish tradition – note it down because one day it may well fall into place. You may not find your family indeed sprang, say, from Charles II, but that an ancestor was a footman or an innkeeper, and if you have remembered a supposed royal connection, your train of thought may lead you to discover that he worked at a royal residence or ran an inn called the *Charles II*.

Circularize your family, especially older members – but set out a query list for them, because this is less trouble to complete, does their thinking for them to a great extent, and will produce what you want rather than what they think to supply. You can always leave a space for them to add whatever else comes to their minds.

If there is an old family Bible, it probably has entries of family events. Are there any papers, certificates, memorial cards, birth announcements, wedding invitations, grave-ownership papers, apprenticeship indentures?

If family details are unknown, check gravestones. Cemeteries are quite helpful, but may charge for searching records and very old ordinary graves are sometimes reorganized for further burials. An ordinary grave as opposed to a private one is a common grave, which will not be marked by individuals' memorial stones.

Whenever at a loss to know where to search when a locality seems to fail, look at a map and extend your area for a radius of five miles. If this fails, extend to ten miles, but beyond that is to become too vague.

DRAWING TREES

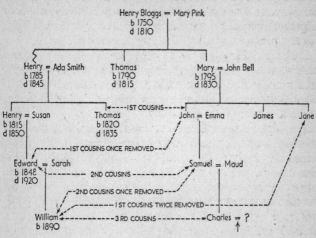

Fig. 1

Compile a family tree, however small. This can be done in various ways, three of which are illustrated here.

In the first, most traditional way, all members of one generation share a common level – with possible variation in complicated cases – and thus relationships are readily seen. There is also room for brief notes on individuals.

The sign = denotes a marriage and ⚮ an illegitimate birth. ⊼ means that not all children have been noted. Perhaps one of the clearest ways to depict children of an individual's different marriages is to number the line, thus:

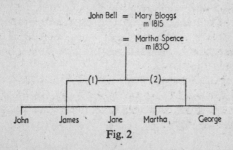

Fig. 2

The second style emphasizes the overlapping of lives and passage of time, which is a useful guide to average lifespans and for easy calculation of such things as likely marriage or possible fatherhood. (See Fig. 3.)

	1700s										1800s										
	50	55	60	65	70	75	80	85	90	95	00	05	10	15	20	25	30	35	40	45	50
Henry Bloggs 3	–	–	–	–	–	–	–	–	–	–	–	–	–	–							
Henry Bloggs 2														–	–	–	–	–	–		
Thomas Bloggs 2								–	–	–	–	–	–	–							
Mary Bloggs											–	–	–	–	–	–	–				
Henry Bloggs 1														–	–	–	–	–	–	–	–
Thomas Bloggs 1														–	–	–	–	–	–	–	

Fig. 3

Parents	Grandparents	Great-Grandparents	Great-Great-Grandparents
Edward Bloggs	Henry Bloggs 1	Henry Bloggs 2	Henry Bloggs 3
			Mary Pink
		Ada Smith	Thomas Smith
			Ellen Good
	Susan Green	George Green 1	George Green 2
			Emily —
		Hannah Jones	James Jones
			Emma Wood
Sarah Black	Stephen Black 1	Stephen Black 2	Stephen Black 3
			—
		Mary Roberts	Edward Roberts
			Martha Young
	Sarah Wills	John Wills	James Wills
			Susan Dunn
		Jane Stone	Thomas Stone
			—

Fig. 4

The third style is that of a simple birth brief or main thread from generation to generation. (See Fig. 4.)

COUSINSHIPS

If two brothers or sisters each have offspring then the children of the one are first cousins to those of the other. If a further generation is born then the one group of grandchildren are second cousins to the other group, and so on. Each difference in *generation* is termed 'removed', so the children on one side and the grandchildren on the other side are first cousins once removed.

ACCEPTABLE EVIDENCE

By now you may have had some surprises, possibly finding a skeleton in a cupboard – what family has no skeleton somewhere? – and perhaps have covered basically quite a number of years. Even so dates should be authenticated, and the following chapters will help with where and how to search, what to look for, how to link it all together and what trains of thought to adopt, taking into consideration the way people were living at given times, and their social and legal rights and status.

The true genealogist will accept only properly proven legal evidence. Certainly if you should get as far as claiming the right to an established coat of arms, the Heralds' College or Lord Lyon will insist on legal evidence, and this consists of any record in accordance with the law of the land. Such records are all government papers of the time – registrations of births, marriages and deaths, parish-register entries, census returns, wills and other official and legal records, padded with bits of side information for interest and to help towards the next real step.

PHONETIC SPELLING

A hazard you will meet very early may be name-spelling. Even nowadays there are people who cannot write, so it is easy to see how spellings of surnames varied when spoken to a clerk who wrote them down phonetically in all good faith, with the additional problems of regional pronunciation and bad copying.

Therefore, in looking through indexes and records generally, a weather eye must be kept open lest something be missed because it is not where anticipated. As an example, take a simple name with its possible forms, remembering that the nearer the beginning of it the variation occurs the more likely it will not spring to the eye automatically, as unconnected surnames will be written in between:

Dixon	Dickon	Dickens
Dixen	Dicken	Dickons
Dickson	Dykon	Dikens
Dicksen	Dyken	Dikons
Dikson	Dicker	Dikkon
Diksen	Dicking	Diccon
Dyxon	Dikon	Dikkons
Dyxen	Diken	Diccons
Dyckson	Dyckon	Diccen
Dycksen	Dycken	Dykkon
Dykson	Deacons	Dickers
Dyksen	Deacon	Decon

etc., and even in one case Tegon! There are even present-day cases of brothers bearing different surnames.

Changes of place-names, particularly abroad, should also be kept in mind, and remember that some places are not always correctly referred to: Kingston-upon-Hull, for instance, is often quoted merely as Hull. If a place-name is not unique ensure you have the correct location.

Never try to cut corners for the sake of speed, or you may have to search a record again later. Look for every imaginable form of spelling. A good book on etiquette will show pronunciations differing from spellings, maybe over a thousand. The most famous probably are Marchbanks for Marjoribanks, Mannering for Mainwaring and Chumley for Cholmondely, which underlines the possibilities in phonetic spelling.

FORENAMES

These have their uses. Forenames may indicate foreign blood; they are sometimes politically motivated, as when Jacobites pointedly used 'James' after James II was deposed in 1688 and shunned 'George' when the Hanoverians ascended the throne in 1714; they often reflect religious beliefs, as when Puritans adopted Praise-be-to-God, Hope, etc. Forenames follow fashions – biblical names were popular once among especially austere Protestants and are traditional with Jews. Tread warily though, because David particularly abounds in Wales and Scotland as well as among Jews. Notice recurring forenames, especially one given persistently to eldest sons and particularly if it is unusual like Sebastian or Ludovick. This may prove to be a signpost, as also may an adapted surname.

There are pitfalls, however. In generations subject to high infant mortality, two or even more brothers may have borne the same forename – even two living simultaneously. This can account for a man being younger or older than anticipated. There may be confusing Latinization – Harriet into Henrietta or Peggy into Margaretta. (See Martin, *Record Interpreter*, which also covers translations of trade surnames.)

In the nineteenth century dual- or multi-forenames were legion, often incorporating a surname – very useful for identification if it is that of, say, a baby's grandmother.

SURNAMES

Family name origins are somewhat too ancient for the average genealogist but they constantly arouse interest. Sometimes servants adopted their medieval master's name, or a woman's was used, either because she was of higher birth than her husband or because she was widowed near the birth of her child. This did not always signify illegitimacy, particularly as there was once no taint attached to that.

A surname may illustrate trade (Carpenter, Mason, Smith); description (Little, Redhead, Quick); locality (York, Ford, Brook); relationship (Johnson, Macdonald, O'Keefe); alternatively it can commemorate some incident or have been a nickname. Compound surnames evolve from family alliances, but may exist only through seeking status rather than coupling property, particularly with common names. Incidentally, for an unusual surname it can be worthwhile to approach subscribers listed in current telephone directories, especially in a relevant area. Many a gap has been filled this way.

CHANGES OF NAME

A man may have changed his name for: inheritance; clarity (Tighe to Tye); Anglicization (Kaminsky to Kaye); profession (acting?); vanity (Smelley to Sweet). If alteration is suspected check the various methods listed below. There is no actual legal necessity to record a change: it need only be exclusively adopted, but this risks complications regarding inheritance, for example. Otherwise alterations could have been by:

> private Act of Parliament: records printed and at the House of Lords Record Office, numerous for the nineteenth century and early 1900s;
> royal licence: records at the College of Arms and at the PRO from late 1600s;
> deed poll: records at the PRO;
> statutory declaration before a justice of the peace or commissioner for oaths (only since 1901);
> advertising: see *London Gazette* and prominent national or local newspapers at public libraries.

Note that aliens cannot change their names under British law without royal licence or Home Office permission.

FAMILY BRIC-À-BRAC

Despise nothing which may have been kept such as old photographs, paintings, miniatures, letters, newspaper cuttings, rent books and the like. Any or all may yield useful clues. Heirlooms may be anything from a thimble or a spoon upwards, and often may indicate how affluent a family was: no working-class housewife was likely to have engraved silver. A family cabinet-maker probably branded his work underneath.

A trip to the local library can settle pretty accurately what year a picture was produced by noting a hairstyle, the cut of a coat, the pattern on material, the jewellery worn, and how – all equally relevant for men and women. One must allow for older people clinging to past fashion and provincial areas sometimes lagging behind the capital.

Below is a sample of fashion changes covering a mere seventy years or so.

	MEN	WOMEN
1830s	Grey or white top hats. Hair fairly long, brushed forward over ears ('door knockers'). Clean-shaven but later modest whiskers. White or black stocks, tall collars. Low-cut single-breasted waistcoats with fob seals. Shirt cuffs turned back over coat sleeves. Swallowtail coats. Tight trousers strapped under boots. Fur or velvet collared short overcoats, long-waisted and full-skirted. Cloaks. Tasselled canes.	Large straw poke bonnets tied under chin, with ribbons or flowers (lace/linen bonnets indoors if married). Hair high at back, centre-parted, ringlets and forehead bandeaux. Velvet cloaks, full collars. Richly coloured dresses. Waists high at first, then at natural level and tiny. Wide sleeves, bows galore, frilled or ruched full skirts, bodices tight and up to wide collars, or else very low. Elbow mittens, long gloves. Wide stoles and shawls. Extra-long muffs. Heavy bracelets and rings, velvet wristbands and later Indian bracelets.
1840s	Moustaches and side whiskers. Smaller stocks. Frock coats.	Headcaps worn at the back, smooth hair, small buns. Flowing veils to waist.

MEN	WOMEN
Mildly checked, looser trousers.	Crossover bodices, transparent bishop sleeves and wider skirts.
	Skirts open waist–hem to reveal dress beneath.

	MEN	WOMEN
1850s	First bowler hats (rare). Much fuller whiskers. Black coats with white trousers, some side-braided. Big cloaks. Tartan plaids.	Smaller bonnets, worn towards the back, large round straw hats. Late in this decade, plain hair, scalloped jackets with wide-ended sleeves. Crinolines of varying proportions and five- or six-tier flounced skirts. Long cloaks, enormous shawls. Tartan much in evidence.
1860s	Stovepipe hats. Very full whiskers – mutton chops, Newgate fringes, flowing beards. Coloured waistcoats, cable watch chains. Pegged trousers. Heavy walking sticks.	Boat-shaped and pork-pie hats. In hair: flowers, bows, streamers. Short jackets. Looped overskirts revealing striped petticoats. Vivid tartans, loud checks, ostrich feathers, tassels. Mannish coats, often buttoned waist–neck, white-collared and large bow ties. Deep-fringed shawls.
1870s	Bowler hats. Moustaches but not whiskers. Neckties with lower collars. Gold Albert watch chains. Plus-four trousers. Heavy Ulster overcoats.	Chignons, high-dressed hair. Bustles. Sham diamond jewellery. Sweeping skirts.
1880s	Bowler hats common. Heavy moustaches – cavalry, waxed, waterfall, upcurled. Beards worn only by Navy, clergy and unconventional. Celluloid collars/cuffs (winged collars with frock coats). Fold-over ties (some coloured shirts with black ties).	Small tilted hats and boaters. Chignons and later short hair. Starched blouses with leg-of-mutton or bishop sleeves. Men's collars, ties and waistcoats. Divided skirts. Smaller muffs. Japanese paper parasols.

MEN	WOMEN
Short double-breasted overcoats.	

1890s	Blazers.	Hats ornamented with birds, flowers, fruit.
	Striped trousers.	Tight veils caught at back, often spotted.
	Coloured socks.	Hair dressed high, tight curls.
	Brown and white shoes.	Hour-glass figures with winged sleeve tops and long-waisted, caped coats.
		Fur capes, feather boas.

Look at pictures' backgrounds, since architecture or furniture may be visible and various types of backcloth passed in and out of favour. This quite often helps in determining by what time someone was still alive or perhaps his identity, while such items as stocks and boots indicate social status. Photographic processes and painting styles can also be dated.

SOCIAL HISTORY

Some national events had a direct effect on the lives of ordinary people. In doing your research bear these in the back of your mind, supplementing them with regional and local events culled from published memoirs, local and trade histories, old newspapers and so on, and try to imagine how your own family would have been affected. Was there a shipping slump in the port where your ancestor was a ship-chandler and could this have caused his bankruptcy or his unexpected presence in the workhouse? Could that cholera epidemic have brought about a woman's early death? Could the hearth tax help in tracing a family home? Could James the grocer actually have been press-ganged into the army? In all sorts of ways you can collect scraps of information of varied importance and use each piece as a stepping stone.

Equipped then with everything you can glean from relatives and your own memory, methodically noted and subdivided, begin tackling the not-so-formidable research in earnest.

WARNING

Periodically press advertisements appear offering plaques depicting family coats-of-arms and they invite inquirers to look up their surnames in the advertisers' books on heraldry. If you want to be authentic, do not be duped by this; remember, sharing the name of an illustrious family does not automatically mean relationship to it. Undoubtedly these firms have all the genuine designs, but the vital ingredient is missing: they cannot possibly say whether your family is entitled to heraldic arms assigned to those who merely happen to share the same name. Of course, if you do establish a right to armorial bearings then that is different. Alternatively you could design a simple crest for yourself, so long as you did not claim it as an official coat-of-arms.

Each individual will find his own route to follow through available information, often interweaving records from different sources, often dodging forward a little in order to know where to step back again. It is for him to decide how to make one record help another so as to use further facilities and extend his tree. The following chapters set out the main sources available.

CHAPTER TWO

CIVIL REGISTERS AND OVERSEAS RECORDS

Civil registration of milestones in individuals' lives was introduced at varying dates during the nineteenth century, so this period is normally simple to trace. Information may also be compiled from what census returns are available to researchers (see Chapter Three).

ENGLAND AND WALES

Somerset House is world famous as the home of population registration, but in fact it houses much more than this. At the end of 1973 many of the General Register Office (i.e. Somerset House) records were physically transferred to St Catherine's House. The GRO is a mine of information, and here you must start your research proper. It is advisable to obtain from this office copies of all birth, marriage and death certificates for your family from 1 July 1837, when registration began. You can get your copies either by personal search of register indexes or by post, and you need to supply basic details or at least a good approximation. Ideally for a birth certificate you should supply forenames, surname *at birth* (which may have changed), day, month, year and place of birth, full name and surname of father, father's occupation, mother's maiden name.

All these details may not be known, but as much as possible should be supplied.

It should also be remembered that it is possible to obtain two kinds of birth certificate: a full one, which gives all the points just mentioned including full address of birthplace, plus the informant's identity, address and either their signature or the fact that that person could not write; a short certificate, which is practically useless to a genealogist because of its prime (though not only) aim of protecting the illegitimate from the revelation of parentage. If a photocopy of the full certificate shows the signature, this may indicate whether the individual was used to writing frequently and at length or not, possibly how well educated he was and also some of his characteristics, for instance, if he was flamboyant. From this you may get an idea of the person's own social status because compulsory education was not introduced until 1870 and before 1891 a man had to pay to educate his children, so perhaps he enjoyed enlightened opinion if he thought education desirable. Thus you begin applying knowledge of the state of society or the law at a given time. On the other hand I have encountered a record of a clerk who inexplicably merely 'put his mark'.

For marriage certificates, endeavour to supply forenames and surname for the groom, forenames and surname *applicable immediately before ceremony* for the bride, marriage date and place.

A marriage certificate may only say 'over twenty-one' – though even this may be useful – but will very likely give ages, if only proving to be an indication. In one case I know of the bride was older than the groom, so she declared a reduced age; and he (perhaps suspecting he was her junior) increased his, so keep an open mind. Certificates also give marital status – showing if it was a second marriage for either party – as well as occupations, current residences, names and surnames of both parties' fathers and fathers' occupations. All this is obviously immensely helpful, and equally so may be names of witnesses, who very likely are relatives. Again, it will be evident whether a marriage took place according to religious rite or civil ceremony, and if the former then whether by licence or banns. The importance of this detail will appear later in this book.

For death certificates again ideally you need forenames and surname at death, date and place of death (not necessarily the deceased's residence), age, occupation, marital status. Certificates give cause of death, which might be useful to have, plus the informant's name, address and relationship, if any. In the cause column may appear 'fourteen days certified', indicating that the deceased was under medical care for that period of time at least.

For births, marriages and deaths registered since 1969 different certificates have been designed. Those for births now state birthplaces of both parents as well as the child, together with any previous surnames of the mother apart from her maiden name, plus any additional name given to the child at, for example, baptism. Marriage certificate details are unchanged, but death certificates now state date and place of birth of the deceased.

Sometimes individuals are touchy about occupations, so be prepared for a man describing himself as a farmer to prove in fact to have been merely an agricultural worker, because even in a small community where everyone knows everyone else, a registrar aware of the truth is still obliged to note down details as given.

Certificates may indicate religious persuasion, because while many people using a place of worship may not actually practise the religion it is certainly indicative if a ceremony took place according to Catholic, Quaker or Jewish rites, for example.

Relationships can be misleading, so keep an open mind as you progress with *all* your research.

Terms vary with period, social background, local usage and personal preference. For instance, 'son' may mean natural son, stepson, son-in-law or even son-in-law of a wife who has been previously married. Grandchildren are sometimes referred to as nephews, and nephews as cousins, while cousins themselves may well not be first cousins. 'Kinsman' can mean almost anything. The description 'natural son' does not imply illegitimacy, but is merely a reliable reference to the son being acknowledged as the man's own.

In genealogical research, civil servants are usually helpful, and sometimes the vaguest details suffice. At the GRO, fees payable have only been increased three times since 1837. Confirmation of a correct reference is cheaper but obviously this is not usually adequate.

When attending St Catherine's House in person, complete

the appropriate form as fully as possible – you will see directions displayed – and then search the index volumes. These are on shelves and are provided with stout leather grips which are essential because of the books' weight. Using the table provided, you search, quite possibly fail, return the volume to its correct place, try the one next to it, and so on. A few volumes later you will find yourself almost sorry you started because of the effort involved. There is no seating, because that would be virtually useless, as the vast majority of people would be continually sitting down and getting up again.

The volumes are ranged in date order by quarter years, that is the quarters of *registration* and not necessarily the event, particularly regarding births. It follows that you may see not only a mere fraction of the alphabet in a volume but also that the year will be divided into March, June, September and December. Therefore if researching a death in April you need the June book for the surname, initial and the year, of course, and if the death was at the end of June it may not have been registered until July (September quarter). Births are given forty-two days' leeway for registration, although nowadays usually an official attends a hospitalized mother promptly. Even stillbirths have to be registered, which can be useful because a known later healthy birth must have occurred at least some months later, even if it was premature. Also an illegitimate baby who is legitimized by the later marriage of its parents may be re-registered. Obviously the details on a birth certificate lead to a marriage, then that marriage in its turn to two births, and so on.

When registration was introduced in 1837 there were inevitably some omissions for various reasons, and there were even some comparatively recently, but by and large the GRO is reliable. Like parish registers (Chapter Four) the most reliable registrations are marriages because people are anxious to prove children are legitimate. Records of deaths, too, are trusty from 1873 because without a certificate, normal burial or cremation is impossible.

However it might easily happen that, perhaps because of lack of prior information, the entry you want is one of several. This could be decided by the actual certificate, because when you find a likely index entry you see only the full name and locality, which may be common to more than one person, though for deaths after 1870 age is also included.

Marriages are decidedly easier to confirm since these are indexed under *both* surnames, so when you have found a likely Robert Foster, say, check the corresponding volume for his bride Emily Preston, and if the reference does not match, then start again. Remember an individual may have married more than once.

If you know of only one marriage party then it is very risky without an uncommon name to assume you have the right reference, but here again the certificate will very likely be the decider. For future reference always note what volumes have been searched and what entries were seen for your surname.

Certificates will be provided only if they appear to tally with the details given, and if they do not then you will be advised. You will be given a receipt when you pay, and can either call back next day to receive the certificate in exchange or have it posted to you, which takes anything from a day to three weeks, depending on the volume of work.

It is possible to ask the GRO to provide certificates for all the entries relating to one surname for a given period (known as a block search), which can be helpful but also rather expensive. However the office is unwilling to do this if it covers a long period or a common name.

In England and Wales district registries have duplicate records covering their own localities; but for genealogists the GRO is a far better source, because it covers all England and Wales and all families have changed locality at some time.

If adoption features in your research, then inquiries in that direction may well be difficult. Naturally it has been the official aim to protect both the adopted child and its adoptive parents, and this is done with a good deal of efficiency.

At the GRO London there is a special Register of Adoptions. This gives birthdate, adoptive parents, court of adoption involved and adoption order date – all these in the adoptive names, of course. Inquirers may apply to that court for permission to see the registration of birth in the original name, but it is impossible to say at random whether or not this would be granted even if the inquirer were the now-adult adopted child himself. In any event, all this hinges on the adoptive name being known. Conversely it could be that sufficient details were known for accurate probing regardless and recent legislation has made tracing easier.

Inquiries regarding divorce are directed to Somerset House.

SCOTLAND

Registration commenced only on 1 January 1855. Application should be made to the Scottish GRO, and (yet unlike England and Wales) the original registration books can be consulted here. See Society of Genealogists (Chapter Six).

IRELAND

For marriages in both Northern Ireland and Eire (except Roman Catholic) from 1 April 1845 to 31 December 1863 as well as for births, marriages and deaths for any date from 1864 to 1921 apply to the GRO, Dublin. Apply there also for a location in Eire from 1922 onwards, but otherwise to the GRO, Belfast. See Society of Genealogists (Chapter Six).

ISLE OF MAN

Contact the Registrar General in Douglas.

AT SEA

The Marine Register Book at the GRO London covers births and deaths at sea since 1 July 1837. This is extremely useful for tracing emigrants. For seamen's deaths 1886–9 consult the PRO Monthly Lists of Deaths of Seamen and Registers of Seamen's Deaths Classified by Cause for 1882–8. The PRO also holds Registers of Births, Marriages and Deaths of Passengers at Sea, which cover 1854–83 for all three occurrences, births and deaths only 1883–7 and deaths only from 1888. Again, all three events are contained in the records classification Ships' Official Logs from 1902. This office also has Registers of Births of British Nationals at Sea and Registers of Deaths of British Nationals at Sea from 1874. See also seafaring in Chapter Eight and overseas records below.

ARMY

Army returns at the GRO London include marriages, as well as births and baptisms of soldiers' children. In some instances these records go back to 1761, though in general to 1790. Almost all military papers anywhere are listed by regiments, so if you are unaware which regiment is involved you will have to do some allied research first. For example, you may be able to discover the regiment from monthly returns in War Office records at the PRO or from making use of some snippet of family tradition (see Chapter Eight, military).

Unfortunately many years ago fire destroyed a great quantity of records referring to serving soldiers. However for 'other ranks' who received discharge certificates – by being pensioned or buying their discharges or completing their terms of service – you can discover details of births, marriages and children from 1756 to thirty years ago. Also see Chapter Eight and overseas records below.

ROYAL AIR FORCE

RAF returns are at the GRO London, but because the RAF is a much younger force they date only from 1920. The name of the unit is necessary. See also Chapter Eight and overseas records below.

OVERSEAS

It is not compulsory for a Briton abroad to register with the British consul a birth, marriage or death which occurs there, but if this has been done then it will appear in the GRO's Consular Returns. However these returns date only from July 1849. (See also Chapter Four.)

Maybe you are interested in events overseas relating to other than British individuals, and indeed for either you may wish to make inquiries abroad. The composition of the Commonwealth is ever-changing and has been so to a greater or lesser degree ever since its inception. Also some countries both of the Commonwealth and elsewhere are so large or administered in such a way that official records are divided into regions, while some islands are grouped together. Not all records are equally complete, detailed or accessible, and it must be remembered that a number of places, both countries and cities, have changed their names.

Initial application for guidance should be made to the relevant country's high commission or embassy in London, the address of which is available at any local public library or at main post offices. A list covering the most likely places of interest is given at the end of this book and any of these offices will direct you to records relating to your case.

Legislation is awaited to move all birth, marriage and death *registers* to the PRO, with microfilms of those over 100 years old available for scrutiny – a great boon for researchers, presently able only to see *indexes*! Later registers will remain at the GRO, but indexes alone on show.

CHAPTER THREE

CENSUS RETURNS

Much of the nineteenth century is also covered by census returns, which are records of the population from differing viewpoints. They are used to count heads, and also to study population movement, trades distribution, family sizes, age group proportions, housing requirements, and so on, and these will be quite invaluable to you.

Leaving aside the very special format of the Domesday Book and certain others, the first official national census in England and Wales is dated 1801. The earliest normally considered useful to a genealogist is that of 1841, but contrary to widespread belief earlier ones are highly informative. Although those for 1931 were destroyed by fire and 1941 was omitted for war reasons, census returns have been updated every ten years, and people have been obliged to answer varying personal questions. All this has been subject to a government pledge of secrecy, resulting in returns being made available to researchers only after a minimum lapse of one hundred years. The 1871 returns were available only in 1973.

There is still controversy about releasing census information, as people fear an invasion of their privacy. However it is impossible to obtain even the smallest item of information from a census for at least seventy years – and thereater until general release it is only in very limited form with special permission from the GRO after stringent conditions have been fulfilled.

Census returns for England and Wales can be examined at the Public Record Office, where for all records you will need a reader's ticket, valid for five years and renewable thereafter. Searches may be undertaken by the PRO on behalf of inquirers, but naturally fees are charged and these may be rather high. Photocopying services are offered, and books or microfilms may be ordered by telephone or letter provided you can quote the appropriate reference, so first get that by a visit or from the official guide.

You will be surprised how crowded places of this kind become, especially in lunch-hours and in the tourist season. If you wish to use a typewriter or tape-recorder there are special sections set aside for these in all PRO rooms. Go armed with plenty of well-sharpened pencils, as no ink or ballpoint pens are permitted for fear of documents being marked. Absolutely forbidden are noise, smoking, drinking and all forms of eating. These regulations apply to most repositories.

As usual you will find the staff extremely helpful and knowledgeable. The clerk in charge will show you index volumes for finding the reference needed, according to which census is of interest. This means that – unless you are keen enough to search a whole area, as I did once for Newcastle-upon-Tyne which has a population of many tens of thousands – you need a fair idea of the locality, i.e. town or parish and if possible the hundred (a county sub-district, also called a wapentake or ward). You may be lucky enough to be researching a town or city which has been catalogued by streets, as has London, but remember street names and even more so house numbers developed gradually.

Your record will be either a book or a microfilm. If a book, it will be divided into small areas summarized at the beginning of each section, so it helps to have a town map or street guide – impossible really for a rural area, of course. If it is a microfilm the same applies, but you will probably need help from a clerk when first using the viewing apparatus. Be warned that census returns, like so many records, are pretty eye-straining and altogether research is a very tiring job. These particular records are handwritten and can be difficult to decipher partly because of poor or old-fashioned writing and partly because they have often faded.

Under 7 June 1841 you will find your household, and the first entry will be the head followed by his family, relatives, visitors and servants. The ruling factor is those who were resident at that address that night. Details given will be name (you have to hope the head of the house gave this fully and accurately), age, sex, occupation and whether or not their birth was in the same county. While useful, this is only of limited help. Ages in 1841 had to be given merely to within five years, except for children up to the age of 15, so if someone was 40–45 they stated 40 – which is vital to bear in mind. Occupation was often glamorized, so should be taken with a pinch of salt. If a woman said she was born in the same county it may not help much, and if she said she was not it helps hardly at all. There is no indication of relationship of one person to another or even if they are married or single, so a couple may be husband and wife, father and daughter, brother and sister, etc.

However you have probably looked already with more joy at the census of 1851 (30 March), 1861 (7 April) or maybe 1871 (2 April). These give not only names but sex, exact age, relationship to the head, and birthplace, as well as occupation. Do not rely, however, on everything being foolproof: memories varied even on age. Still, it can be useful to be assured a person was female if their Christian name was, say, Julian, Hilary, Evelyn or Maud – but then many a surname used as a forename presents this hazard.

Note everything fully and carefully, even a meaningless squiggle since it may prove important later. A single line ruled across the page indicates the completion of entries for a family, while a double line indicates completion of a whole household. In birthplaces, 'I' means Ireland, 'S' Scotland and 'F' foreign parts. Scotland may be entered as 'North Britain'. 'j' signifies a journeyman in any given trade, which means a man who had completed an apprenticeship but was not a master. A farmer may be shown as owning such-and-such amount of land or so many cows. The servants in a house will indicate the householder's social standing. Census returns not only help greatly in leading on to the previous generation through ages and birthplaces, but also throw considerable light on the times. You will find servants as young as seven years old maybe, or a pit boy even younger.

1841

ADDRESS	NAME	AGE	OCCUPATION	WHETHER BORN IN SAME COUNTY
Mutford	William Mills	35–39	Shoemaker	Yes
	Louisa Mills	35–39		Yes
	George Mills	18	Bricklayer's Labourer	Yes
	William Mills	13	—	Yes
	Samuel Mills	11	—	Yes
	Amos Mills	3	—	Yes

1851

ADDRESS	NAME	RELATIONSHIP TO HEAD OF HOUSEHOLD	STATE	AGE	OCCUPATION	PLACE OF BIRTH
102 Mill Road Mutford	William Mills	Head	Married	48	Shoemaker Waterman	North Cove, Suffolk
	Louisa Mills	Wife	Married	48	—	Mutford, Suffolk
	Samuel Mills	Son	Unmarried	20	Shoemaker Journeyman	Mutford, Suffolk
	Annah Mills	Daughter	Unmarried	2	—	Mutford, Suffolk

Fig. 5 Census particulars showing the details available at different times and their uses, compiled from Crown copyright records in the Public Record Office, London, references HO 107/1030/5 and HO 107/1805/227

The entries in Fig. 5 refer to a village, but for a town, having the fuller address might have been even more helpful, particularly if there was a chance of title deeds being involved, and it would be nice anyway to be able to visit the actual site and maybe the actual house. As regards the individuals of course ages become much more precise and later entries even bear out earlier ones, but not always so. Also, births are recorded before the establishment of the GRO. Note incidentally that young William was not the apparent eldest son, though bearing his father's forename, so there may have been an earlier boy who had died.

By 1851 George Mills was twenty-eight and no longer at home. Young William in fact had also left. Both could have died meanwhile. Remembering the earlier census was taken in June and the later in March, very probably Samuel was just about to come of age and had followed his father in trade. Amos is missing in 1851, and it would be worth checking at the GRO to see if he had died. At any rate the later return shows he was not William and Louisa's youngest child and there are likely to have been some between Amos and Annah.

In 1841 it can be surmised that the six people were the father, mother, and their four children, but it would not be impossible for them to be a widower, his sister and her sons, so if your research allows, try to verify relationships with a later census or other documents. Never take anything for granted.

It will be noticed, too, that the elder William was not only a shoemaker but also a waterman. Perhaps he plied a little ferrying trade across the river to augment his income. His name may have been known from a son's marriage certificate, but that certificate would not have mentioned his wife – except possibly as a witness and without giving her relationship. The census also shows that the elder William was still alive in March 1851, which narrows the search for his death and maybe his will.

Lastly, far from being encumbered with searching for origins throughout East Anglia one could now confine oneself to North Cove for the father and, hopefully, his forebears. The smaller the location and the further back in time, the more likely a family has stayed at least more or less locally for generations.

For Scottish census returns apply to the Scottish GRO. For Ireland there are very few of these returns (complete and available for 1901 and 1911, with parts back to 1659) but they can be found at the PRO of Ireland.

The PRO in London houses returns for New South Wales dated November 1828. These are in alphabetical order by inhabitants, state age, whether free of bond, ship and year of arrival, criminals' sentences, religion, occupation, residence and details of any land or stock ownership. It is a great pity more such records do not exist for other areas and dates.

So now, with the GRO and the census returns, backed by personal and family documentation or memories, you are well on your way to putting down the roots of your family tree. But do not go on to the next generation yet: a pause to round off the current one may save a great deal of time and trouble later. Remember to keep to one surname – persevere with your Smiths and let the Joneses and Robinsons they married wait awhile.

Then take time out to extend the family tree and study it to see what clues it offers. Begin to enter notes under the headings of individuals in your family in your loose-leaf book. Use your imagination and memory to work out your next moves. If you have a shoemaker or a waterman on your list make it your business to discover if he could possibly have been a farrier, making shoes for horses, and what alternative trades watermen could follow, since two occupations may not seem at first sight to go together.

At this stage, you will be able to integrate many of your fragments of information and perhaps piece together whole generations or sections of them. Using the two sources of certificates and returns in conjunction you may well be able to solve the puzzle of someone's age or establish more exactly when a man died, since a wife may appear in later census returns as a widow. From 1851 returns will also show all the children in a family at home that night, who then may be checked on at the GRO for residences at different times, for example. Also, the apparent status of a man can often determine whether or not he was likely to leave a will. Individuals may be missing due to illness, death, work, boarding school, imprisonment, etc.

CHAPTER FOUR

PARISH AND SIMILAR RECORDS

PARISH REGISTERS

With the GRO and census returns having taken you back to 1837, and further at least in gauging earlier dates, now is the time to turn to both ecclesiastical and lay local records. Wills and other documents, applicable to both before and after this date, will probably help too, but for convenience we shall deal with these each in their own right.

Most people find parish registers have a romance about them, especially when handling the real thing rather than a copy. There is something special about old-fashioned script on aged parchment, though not all registers are like that. Although they are not all kept together, this can be an advantage in many ways. Again, you need to check which parish covered your area at the time, since a more modern parish may have been created subsequently and so will not have old enough registers. (See heading 'boundaries' in this chapter.)

Whereas the GRO deals with births, church records are concerned with baptisms, although sometimes birthdates are mentioned additionally, and baptism may occur at any time from birth to years later, or not at all. Elizabethan children were usually baptized when three days old. If years have elapsed it is often useful to try to find a likely reason – maybe war, religious differences, some sort of domestic trouble such as parents' illness – but of course the cause may remain a mystery. Similarly, churches record burial, not death, though often registers will show the date of death, too, and obviously burial cannot be delayed long. Marriages naturally were recorded at the time, supplemented by marriage banns and licences.

The earliest parish recording is 1538 but not all records

survived. Although you can see parish records even up to the present time, the final practical date is 1837 when the GRO takes over. Many parish records have been printed, though some stop at 1812 because at the time the information was becoming too recent for people then alive not to object to its publication. These are both easier to read and more readily available; but entries should be checked against originals in case of copying errors.

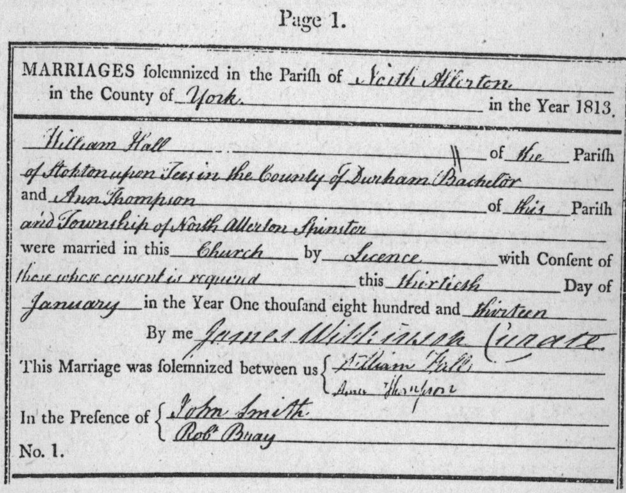
Page 1.

MARRIAGES ſolemnized in the Pariſh of North Allerton in the County of York in the Year 1813.

William Hall of the Pariſh of Stockton upon Tees in the County of Durham Bachelor and Ann Thompson of this Pariſh and Township of North Allerton Spinster were married in this Church by Licence with Conſent of those whose consent is required this thirtieth Day of January in the Year One thouſand eight hundred and thirteen

By me James Wilkinson Curate

This Marriage was ſolemnized between us { William Hall / Ann Thompson

In the Preſence of { John Smith / Robt Bray

No. 1.

Fig. 6 Extract from a parish register

When researching a register, never take it for granted that an entry with the same name relates to the right family – and *always* remember varying spellings of names. Names may also have been changed.

Marriage registers are the most accurate (because the ceremony legitimized the children), followed by death registers. Records of baptism are the least important because not everyone is baptized.

In Queen Anne's time (1702–14) marriages were often bargains struck by parents in the upper and middle classes, although there were many runaway romances ending in marriage. Because it was considered humiliating for them and their parents if they remained single, girls accepted the system, in spite of the fact that divorce was almost unknown – only six divorces were legalized in this reign, through Church courts and by special Acts of Parliament.

Unless a poor family was involved, arranged marriages (and dowries) were the rule rather than the exception right up to the nineteenth century, frequently merely to legitimize children. In the eighteenth it was common for a bride to be pregnant, so be flexible in gauging a marriage date from a known birth or vice versa.

Most registers are available in some form at the appropriate CRO, but some remain with the individual religious incumbent. A wealth of information on the whereabouts of registers can be seen in the series *National Index of Parish Registers*. Incomplete, eventually it will cover the whole of the United Kingdom and at the time of writing is in print for pre-1974 counties as follows: Vols. 1 and 2, sources of births, marriages and deaths before 1837 (Vol. 2 specializing in Nonconformists); Vol. 3, Roman Catholic and Jewish; Vol. 5, Gloucester, Hereford, Oxford, Shropshire, Warwick and Worcester counties; Vol. 12, Scotland. Due very soon is Vol. 11 (Northumberland and Durham, probably with Yorkshire).

The forerunners of these volumes are still in print, very valuable still and inexpensive. They are *Parish Register Copies*, Part 1, Society of Genealogists Collection and Part 2, Other than Society of Genealogists Collection.

When approaching an incumbent, do enclose at least stamps for a reply. Most clergymen are co-operative, but they are harassed and hardworking, and are also legally entitled to charge fees: many do not, and their generosity should be rewarded. These fees are 30p for the first year searched for baptisms, marriages or burials, with 15p for each subsequent year. Certificates are 50p each.

Entries give various information, occasionally amusing or revealing. You may get useful ages or occupations, or you may be unlucky and get very little and be unable to decide between one entry and another, in which case you hope for a solution from details in a will or some such document.

Around 1762 you will find the father's signature appears in a baptismal register. If he could not write it will be merely 'his mark', but otherwise perhaps his signature can be compared with that in another place and so be a signpost. From 1754, both bride and groom should have signed the marriage register, but they again – especially the bride – may have been illiterate.

CALENDAR CHANGE

Before 1752 there was a Church and legal dating method, which meant that the year began on Lady Day (25 March); then the calendar was reverted to beginning each year on 1 January (this method had been employed until the end of the twelfth century). As a result of this change, the period 1 January to 24 March was shown that year as 1751/2 and for historical purposes this period in preceding years rightly should appear as 1750/1, 1699/1700, etc., although sometimes the terms OS (Old Style) and NS (New Style) are used.

If you read a document relating to, for example, 12 February 1740 then do not be misled, because it would refer to the end of the old-style year 1740 and by modern dating would be in fact early 1741. Naturally, at the time people found it difficult to accept the new system and were irritated by the loss of eleven days, 3–13 September 1752 inclusive, which were omitted to right the calendar after it had become out of tune with the sun.

BANNS, MARRIAGE LICENCES AND BISHOPS' TRANSCRIPTS

If you are unable to trace a marriage then try banns, which became compulsory when Lord Hardwicke's Marriage Act 1753 took effect in 1754, although banns are recorded over very many years before the law insisted on either them or a licence. However from about 1644 until 1660 parish registers were neglected as a result of civil disorder and consequently your research may be affected.

If there are no banns, try to trace a licence (formerly essential if a marriage took place on days of fasting or in Lent but not issued 1641–60) for which the following guide indicates where to apply: if both parties of the same diocese, the bishop; if different dioceses involved in the same province, the archbishop (vicar-general licences); if different provinces (see Chapter Five, 1857 and earlier) are involved, the Faculty Office; if a 'peculiar' (a parish which, briefly, is more or less independent and not answerable in the usual way to a bishop) is involved, the CRO.

Should you have difficulty with any register, then try contemporary copies, because these had to be passed to bishops and are known as bishops' transcripts. They are not always true copies, being sometimes more and sometimes less full than originals. The archivist at the appropriate CRO can give advice if they are not in his own custody.

Diocesan registries may have marriage allegations, which may include bonds from about 1600 to 1823. An allegation is a bridegroom's statement on oath that the marriage did not contravene the law in any way, and if you can find this, it will often give invaluable details such as ages or parents' names.

Bonds, given on behalf of marriage parties, were required before the issue of a licence. These bound the sureties to a fixed cash sum, rather like an alleged offender is allowed free on bail, and also incorporated genealogical details. They are sometimes for fantastic sums, but normally it was just 'paper' money. A library will advise whether an index of allegations and bonds for your particular county has been printed.

There may not be traceable banns or licence, and of course neither guarantees that a marriage was not cancelled or postponed.

Remember that up to 1754 boys could marry at 14 and girls at 12, although now, no one can do so until they are 16, and not until 18 if without consent of parents or guardians. Similarly it used to be forbidden to a greater extent than nowadays to marry certain relatives by blood or former marriage.

NON-PAROCHIAL RECORDS

Members of religious denominations other than the Established Church are also recorded in official parish registers. Their births were included by a law dated 1695 and theoretically their marriages by Lord Hardwicke's Act of 1753, though this latter excluded Quakers and Jews. However the law was often disobeyed, especially by Roman Catholics.

At the same time these Dissenters frequently kept their own records – legally from 1689 – albeit not always covering everything. Apart from many of the Roman Catholic records (which remain with incumbents), these are now in the custody of the PRO London, and cover England and Wales. Included in non-parochial papers are Huguenots and other foreign Protestants, Quakers (Society of Friends), Presbyterians, Independents, Baptists, Wesleyan Methodists and others, as well as those ceremonies which took place at the King's Bench Prison, Fleet Prison, May Fair Chapel, the Mint, Bunhill Fields famous Nonconformist burial ground, and the Lying-in Hospital, Holborn, all in London. The dates applicable, generally speaking, are 1775–1837 but in some cases as early as 1600 and as late as 1857. Perhaps the best are the Quaker records (also with the Society of Friends' Library) and it may be of interest that many tradesmen and professional men of the eighteenth century were Methodists. Also contact the Methodists' Archives & Research Centre. Dr Williams's Library has some Presbyterian, Independent and Baptist registers relating to London, but it is preferable to visit the PRO.

The PRO also holds recordings of vast numbers of secret marriages from 1667 to 1777.

If by any chance you know a baptism, say, took place at Greenwich or the Chelsea Hospital or at a Chapel Royal or Somerset House Chapel, or if you find links with any foreign Protestant church or the Russian Orthodox Church, you should approach the PRO.

JEWS

Members of the Jewish race were banished from England from 1290 until about 1660. Thereafter, exceptionally fine records exist of births, marriages and deaths, which are more detailed than the Christian counterparts. Unfortunately none of these are at the PRO, so you should approach the Jewish Historical Society of England or the relevant local synagogue. Remember that Jewish children are named ceremonially at the age of eight days.

WALES

Welsh parish registers and bishops' transcripts are in the National Library of Wales.

SCOTLAND

If your area is Scottish then for Church of Scotland dates before 1855 you will need to contact the Scottish GRO. It would also help to read the highly praised Hamilton-Edwards' *In Search of Scottish Ancestry*.

IRELAND

While Irish parish registers are at the PRO Dublin, an enormous number were lost in the 1922 fire and it hardly helps that the losses related mainly to small rural parishes and were dated merely from early nineteenth century, if it is one of those you need! Help may be forthcoming from the National Library of Ireland, since discoveries can be made by those who are patient, and it is recommended that you read Clare's *A Simple Guide to Irish Genealogy* – though the simplicity of Irish genealogy is a moot point. As far as Northern Ireland goes, appeal to the Ulster-Scot Historical Society, particularly about gravestone inscriptions.

OVERSEAS

Inquiries about India, Pakistan, Burma, Aden, St Helena and many places in South-East Asia should be made to the Foreign & Commonwealth Office. If your family may have been in St Petersburg, Russia (now Leningrad) between 1818 and 1840 then try the records of the Independent Church in that city, which are now in London's PRO. The Bishop of London's registers at Guildhall Library and the Vicar-General's registers at the Faculty Office also deal in part with overseas. Some registers of baptisms, marriages and burials abroad 1706–1939 are available at the Corporation of London Record Office.

PRINTED SOURCES

Your specific locality may be covered by printed lists issued by the Society of Genealogists (see Chapter Six), the Harleian Society, a local parish register society or a local archaeological society. For Roman Catholics contact the Catholic Record Society if you are interested in dates back to 1791, while the Huguenot Society has published indexed volumes of registers up to about 1800 for French Protestants who came to England. The Bunhill Fields register has also been printed. Where possible, request guidance from the reference library of the area concerned.

HANDWRITING

You may be perplexed by handwriting, so you will need to study styles. However, the time may come when the writing and the Latin, Greek, Norman French or even shorthand encountered, are beyond you, and then the wisest course is to seek expert advice. Although medieval Latin (the most widely met language) fell out of use in official papers at varying times from about the end of the fifteenth century, it was still used elsewhere up to 1733. By then some words had become so Anglicized that they are self-explanatory.

Style can date handwriting fairly accurately, but remember to take the writer's age into account. Styles of writing have changed periodically by degrees, not only in phraseology but also in outlines of lettering. One of your biggest challenges will occur when examining parish registers. The art of deciphering ancient writing is known as palaeography, and it is not intended to do more here than indicate basic points as there are reference books on this subject. One recommended is the Society of Genealogists' *Guide to Handwriting*.

It is likely that the first poser will be the old way of presenting the letter s in the long form ſ or ſ, which persisted into the late nineteenth century. It appears clearly in the writing of Charles Dickens and also in the census, though most frequently when a double s is required. A beginner may confuse it with f, but the golden rule is that the f has a line through the stem, whereas the s has one on the left. Up to the eighteenth century, a double ſ at the start of a word denotes a capital letter.

Until quite late i and j were synonymous, with both being used in numerals – as in iij, representing the figure 3. The capital letters I and J are regularly interspersed, well into census-return times, with names such as John presented as Iohn. You will find i, too, being written as y, as in hys (his). The y outline also was adopted as the misrendering of a Saxon sign for the th sound, which accounts for ye instead of the.

If you encounter ə (several periods of time) it will probably be an e – though it must be emphasized that when tussling with old writing it is essential to study the whole alphabetic style of the day, because letters can be confused; and when a substantially different hand is met, practice is the best way to familiarize yourself with it.

Before the adoption of 's for possession, men wrote 'John his son' (John's son).

With any difficult writing there are two basic tenets to observe; compare outlines you cannot read with those you can, and follow any obvious flow of the pen. When several small strokes are involved, count each one and use common sense, e.g. minimum. Hurry through the text and leave gaps,

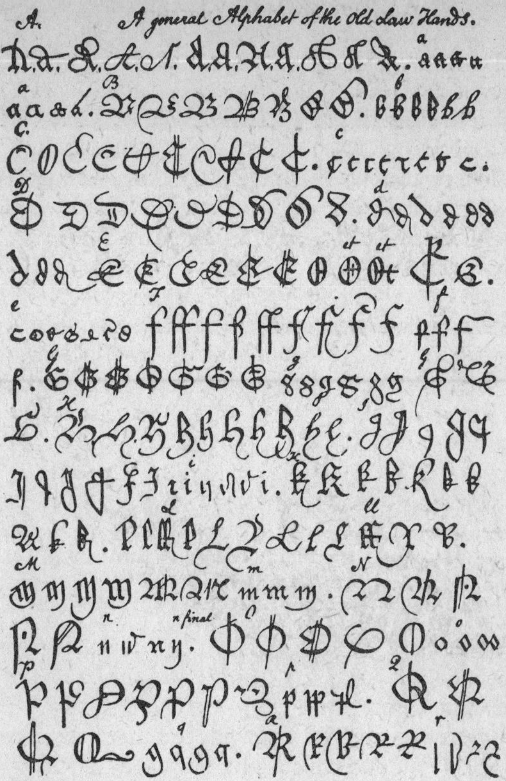

ALPHABETS from A. Wright's *Court Hand Restored* (5th ed., 1818, plates 18, 19), illustrating a variety of forms of letters, mainly but not entirely from 16th and 17th century Legal and Chancery hands.

Fig. 7 Alphabets taken from Wright's *Court Hand Restored*

if you like, retracing more slowly with the resulting aid of context.

Contractions have been used for centuries – indeed once they were the rule rather than not. Frequently they are self-explanatory or can be guessed, though at times choice is governed by context, e.g. yr for your or year. A contraction may well be raised a little, even into late Victorian times, e.g. w^t (with) or addit^n (addition). Earlier writing shortened with a line or curve over a word indicating the omission of m or n, e.g. comīt (commit) or earlier still, with charming vagueness, leaving the missing letters to one's imagination.

Past generations contracted words at their beginnings also, for example:

ꝑ pro
ꝑ per, par or por
ꝑ pre

Always remember that the old may have tutored the young and so youth may pen an outdated hand.

Centuries ago the incumbents of the Established Church's parishes became in effect (along with churchwardens, parish clerks and other officials) local administrators on a multitude of civil matters. Apart from the manor, it was natural for people to look to the Church for guidance and authority and to regard it as a centre not just for worship and pleasure but also for civil organization. It was a very convenient, ready-made structure for government use.

Churchwardens were and still are responsible for keeping accounts connected with the upkeep of the parish church in every respect, so their papers can be helpful if your ancestor was a joiner, sempstress or mason.

Together with the vestry, churchwardens were responsible for regulating and providing relief for the poor, destitute, orphans, foundlings and infirm, as well as dealing with criminals, vagrants, parish apprentices, highways, workhouses and a great many other aspects of day-to-day life. These parish officials appointed various others to oversee hedges, land, water, etc., and were concerned in some measure with any schooling undertaken by the incumbent. In these papers you may find lists of pewholders, details of local charities, collection of Church rates, notes on bastards and foundlings apprenticed to tradesmen, money paid to carters for transporting building materials for church repairs, to washerwomen for laundering church linen or to glaziers for installing windows. Also there should be names of inhabitants vaccinated against smallpox, owners of cattle grazing on Church land, applications (often with valuable genealogical details) for the removal from town or village of a family with no legal right to remain, receipt of tithe payments, and so on. Rating records are arguably the most useful to you, since they usually give at least vague addresses, property values, details of children, etc.

Among registers there may be records of confirmations, last rites, exorcism, excommunication, witchcraft, or punishments for fornication, adultery or bigamy, which could throw some light on your research.

BOUNDARIES

In almost any library can be discovered parish boundaries and addresses – but remember that both parish and diocesan boundaries change from time to time and that often parishes have amalgamated. During World War II a number of churches were bombed and lost their records, in which case apply to the CRO or the diocesan bishop's secretary for the whereabouts of any copies. The local library will also advise on churches in existence at a given date.

County limits themselves have changed, even before 1974. Middlesex, for example, exists no more but until comparatively recently it embraced places as diverse as St John's Wood and Bow. It is necessary to be sure which county applies: there are still a record office and an archaeological society for Middlesex. Likewise 'London' is a term used nowadays to refer to a very wide area, but for historical purposes it should be only the famous square mile of the City of

London, as even Westminster is a separate city in its own right. Radnorshire, too, has been absorbed and new counties have emerged – Cumbria, Humberside and others. In the same way diocesan limits have altered but it should be simple to check at a reference library for the right see for your family's parish.

MONUMENTAL INSCRIPTIONS

Technically, these consist of inscriptions on any kind of monument – war memorials, tombstones, church plaques, brasses, effigies, commemorative windows, memorial chapels, and so on. However, I believe the term would better be 'memorial inscriptions', since this category can include bells, fonts, furniture, chalices and altar cloths expressly there to preserve the memory of individuals who may still have been alive at the time of dedication. For example, my own parish church has an eighteenth-century gallery with ornamentation incorporating the donor's monogram and listing parish benefactions.

In the case of effigies very often a man and wife – frequently with their children, too – will appear together. All their names may be there, or none, and research may be needed to establish whether or not they might be your kin. Maybe a coat-of-arms will have been added or the figure of a favourite animal or an impression of a home. It is likely that an effigy will provide a clear idea of status, date, and possibly occupation, although it will be probably flattering rather than honest in physical portrayal. One of the finest groups must be that in alabaster of the Savage family at Elmley Castle, pre-1974 Worcestershire, representing no less than eight figures and dating from the seventeenth century.

Tombstones in graveyards or cemeteries often list whole families, which is of enormous help in coping with register gaps, caused for instance by a wife returning to her own family for confinements and subsequent baptisms. They sometimes add snippets of information not recorded elsewhere – relief at the silence of a shrew or reference to 'home is the sailor, home from the sea'.

Here is a delightful sample from Lydford in Devon:

Here lies in a horizontal position the outward case of George Routleigh, watchmaker, whose abilities in that line were an honour to his profession. Integrity was the mainspring and prudence the regulator of all the actions of his life. Humane, generous and liberal, his hand never stopped till he had relieved distress. So nicely regulated were all his motions that he never went wrong, except when set agoing by people who did not know his key – even then he was easily set aright. He had the art of disposing of his time so well that his hours glided away in one continual round of pleasure and delight, till an unlucky minute put a period to his existence. He departed this life November 14 1802 aged 57, wound up in the hope of being taken in hand by his Maker and of being thoroughly cleaned and repaired and set agoing in the world to come.

Places which are now towns, cities or suburbs were once villages, at varying dates of course. Conversely, some places once of fair importance have become much less busy commercially.

There has always been a tendency for village families to intermarry. This itself has to be borne in mind, and also if it happened to two families a couple of hundred years ago then local people now with the same name may not even know they are related, the link having become so tenuous. So when you look around a country churchyard (or what was a country churchyard) be *very* careful about taking notes and *very* careful in analysing them. A tombstone which gives a lot of information and seems to be just what you are looking for can refer to the wrong individuals. You should look round for other inscriptions anyway – cover the churchyard – and later at leisure link up whole families. There may be one little detail which shows you have not in fact found what you thought you had found.

CHAPTER FIVE

WILLS

Wills are one of the prime sources of genealogical information, since several family identities, a good idea of a man's position in life and an accurate indication of his residence and possessions can often be gleaned from them. They may also give considerable insight into his general affairs, and certainly mention date of death and value of estate.

A son may have been specifically excluded from benefit and the reason given, but if he was left only a shilling it usually means merely that he had already received his inheritance, perhaps for business. If administration was granted to a creditor it does not necessarily imply bankruptcy.

It may have taken years to prove a will and effect settlement, so you may have a fairly lengthy and complicated search for it. With it may be a bond of tuition or guardianship for children, or a codicil, or between about 1540 and 1740 an inventory of possessions, so inquire about these when making your search. An inventory will give details of furniture, furnishings, clothing, jewellery, plate, cattle, and in fact everything owned, with valuations. Buy a photocopy of a will whenever possible, as this is much easier and more reliable than copying, especially if it is lengthy, and is also useful for comparing signatures.

However, if you wish to take brief notes meantime then list every name mentioned; for the sake of another five minutes' effort you may save yourself endless trouble later. A brother may not appear to warrant attention; but if you have his details and it transpires his name was not just John Smith but John Montague Smith then the Montague may be invaluable in leading you onwards. It could establish whether his father married Mary Robinson or Mary Montague, and of course that means *your* lineage, too. Executors, supervisors and witnesses may have been related to the testator or connected to him through business, beneficiaries years ago being legally able to act as witnesses, too. You should jot down the testator's name and abode, court and date of proving, date of will, names of legatees and details of legacies, with any conditions, names of executors, witnesses and anyone else, relationships and any addresses, and whether signed or merely 'marked'.

Of course, there are many instances where no will was left. There may have been little to leave or, especially in the past when people felt they might be tempting providence, the matter was often left until illness or accident created urgency, when it may have been too late. In that event look for administration bonds (known as 'admons' and listed in probate records immediately after the wills of the appropriate surname initial) which give permission for the disposal of a man's estate when he dies intestate. Then there are such things as depositions or noncupative wills – certified statements of a dying person's wishes merely spoken to witnesses – and there have been cases where wags have treated the subject with brave levity and written their wishes on most unlikely materials, the classic being that written on an egg!

Sometimes a man's will was proved away from his known locality, perhaps because he owned property or carried on business in more than one place or was given to travelling. However, undisputed inheritance frequently passed informally just by an understanding. Yet again, a will can have probate granted by more than one court.

In past centuries women had few rights – an example of social history creeping into your work. Before 1882, generally speaking a woman did not leave a will unless she was a spinster or widow, as everything a wife owned belonged in law to her husband (even herself) and she had no right to dispose of it. Women were given this right by the Married Women's Property Act 1882.

Wills fall into two categories, before and after 1858. Help from the printed word lies in Camp's *Wills & Their Whereabouts* and in Gibson's *Wills & Where to Find Them*, equipped with maps of jurisdictions.

1858 AND LATER

From 11 January 1858 either the original or a copy of every will or letters of administration for England and Wales has been held by the Principal Probate Registry; if a copy, then the original is with the district registry, where you would probably need to make an appointment. The registry will supply photocopies, but you cannot copy a whole will yourself and must be content with noting basic details as mentioned above. Indexes make the whole operation easy.

1857 AND EARLIER

Before the Court of Probate Act 1857 it had been considered that the Church was the most convenient and well organized body to handle will and admon formalities. So for this earlier voluminous category ecclesiastical courts pertain, and their structure is somewhat complicated. This is outlined below, but the records are in many cases now in various depositories other than the original homes, such as with guild or manorial records. Records of Crown-held funds from lawsuits and unsettled wills are among Chancery papers held at the PRO.

England is divided into two Church provinces – Canterbury and York. Canterbury covers the old counties of Shropshire, Stafford, Derby, Lincoln and all points south, while York covers those of Cheshire, Lancashire, Yorkshire, Nottingham and all points north to the Scottish border. These two areas are embraced by the Prerogative Court of Canterbury (PCC) and the Prerogative Court of York (PCY).

PCC, being the senior, was enabled on its own to deal with wills of individuals whose estates were in parts of *both* provinces. Within its own half of the country, too, it coped with wills concerning more than one diocese, and relating to English estates of those who died at sea or abroad. Sometimes PCY area wills were dealt with by the PCC simply for status reasons. PCC records are at the PRO London, and are indexed in manuscript from 1383 to 1858, but for details of these and printed indexes see Camp's *Wills & Their Whereabouts*. (Mr Camp is currently editing *An Index to the*

Wills Proved in the Prerogative Court of Canterbury 1750–1800 for the Society of Genealogists, though based on documents with known imperfections.) Production of some wills for researchers requires three days' notice.

PCY similarly covers multi-diocese and lesser area cases within the northern province and, in partnership with PCC, many involving both provinces. Records are at the Borthwick Institute of Historical Research, York. The staff will undertake to search their extensive indexes and produce a will provided the proving date is known to within five years. Otherwise it is essential to attend personally or to employ a professional researcher. The institute will provide on request a comprehensive résumé of its records.

It should be noted that *all* wills during the Commonwealth Protectorate (1652–60) were proved in the Court of Civil Commission and are among PCC records.

Early wills are rather few, but reach back as far as 1383 and are fairly complete from about 1600. An enormous number have been listed by various societies in their published volumes, so apart from referring to the two important works noted earlier in this chapter, inquire at your library for other printed sources, such as those of the Yorkshire Archaeological Society.

To trace which court is applicable to a given case it is possibly best to start with the lowest and work on to the highest. This means commencing with an archdeaconry or commissary court, or maybe a peculiar (see Chapter Four). If two archdeaconries are involved then approach diocesan records – which in fact cover the bulk of wills – and if still unsuccessful try PCC or PCY. Alternatively work downwards. You can find out about locations at the CRO or you can write direct to the Church body. Whichever way you use, it is not easy: there were 372 courts ruling areas where land was held or a testator died, and a search does not always work out in practice as it should in theory, so it needs to be systematic. Because a man lived, worked and died in Manchester, say, is no guarantee that his will did not go to PCC.

You may be lucky or you may have a long search – and unknown to you there may exist neither will nor admon.

However, most copy wills from the smaller courts, and also the peculiars, are nowadays with CROs. Until the end of the eighteenth century anyone of any real substance (which includes farmers and tradesmen) tended to have his will proved at Canterbury or York as a matter of prestige.

WALES

Pre-1858 Welsh wills and admons are housed in the National Library of Wales.

SCOTLAND

For a Scottish will, inquire at Edinburgh General Register House, and note that the law differs even today. The Scottish equivalent of English probate is confirmation, and it remains necessary to provide an inventory and schedule of debts.

IRELAND

Northern Ireland wills post-1858 are at the Belfast PRO, but for those from 1536 to 1858 they have only indexes, owing to fire losses when wills for all Ireland were in Dublin. Dublin PRO has wills back in some cases to 1708, and the National Library of Ireland is ready to assist researchers. Be warned though that Irish genealogy is difficult.

JEWS

As already stated, Jews were banned from England from 1290 until about 1660. However, there is an alphabetical index of all traceable wills and admons proved in PCC pertaining to Jewish families: see the Jewish Historical Society of England's *Anglo-Jewish Notabilities*, which also has a brief biographical dictionary and a list of Anglo-Jewish coats-of-arms.

INQUISITIONS POST MORTEM

These date from the thirteenth century to 1660 and are kept at the PRO London. Briefly, on the death of a man a tally was made of his holding of Crown land and the services due thereby, and included were the heir's name and age and a history of ownership, so whole pedigrees are often included.

CHAPTER SIX

THE PRINTED WORD

Libraries are indispensable to the genealogist. Many can supply photocopies of their local census returns which in itself is a major service!

You will need to use your imagination applied to your own special case in scanning reference shelves and index cards. There will be special sections devoted to genealogy and heraldry, but also look for a local history section and for general reference books of use to you, such as those on mining or shipowning or the Army or whatever. Among genealogical books will be a number on doing your own research, but beware of their being outdated in some respects, as in recent years records have been moved to different depositories as well as augmented by bequest or discovery, not to say that hours and fees alter.

It cannot be stressed too strongly or repeated too frequently that notes should be taken (and safely kept!) when reading. Never try to cut corners, or you may rue having to go over the same ground again.

At the back of this book is a bibliography designed to provide a basis for research, to which undoubtedly you will soon add for yourself and may even find a book on your own family. General reference books are also very helpful – encyclopaedias, dictionaries covering dates, quotations or Latin, *Whitaker's Almanack*, etc. Then there are studies of surnames dealing with origins and preponderance in different regions or even towns, complemented by those on forenames and their popularity in varying areas at varying times.

Use your library to look up exactly what there is at the PRO London – there are several books on its contents, but perhaps best is HMSO's *Guide to the Contents of the Public Record Office*. If you trace back to the seventeenth century, use your library to check heralds' visitations, which are county-classified recordings of armorial bearings incorporating pedigrees compiled on the spot at the time. Even the most modest family may have sprung from noble stock. If you trace your family to 1700 or so then it was probably either yeoman or in some way connected with the upper classes, and this implies visitation mention.

Your library will have the publications of the Harleian Society, Surtees Society, Parish Register Society and others. If dealing with people of any social standing at all, look in printed volumes of *Gentleman's Magazine* or *Notes & Queries* for announcements of births, marriages and deaths. Use your library to read about monumental inscriptions, coats-of-arms and histories of anything of interest – seafaring, pottery, agriculture, mechanical engineering. Use it to get the 'feel' of a period from contemporary novels by Jane Austen and others of her ilk, or learn from reliable non-contemporary authors who have really studied their period, like Walpole's *Herries Chronicle* or Galsworthy's *Forsyte Saga*.

If relevant see *Directory of Directors, Who's Who, Who Was Who, Burke's Peerage, Burke's Landed Gentry, Debrett,* and so on. There are specialist books, too – professional lists for the different Churches, the law, medicine, etc. – and your man could be in the *Dictionary of National Biography*.

Use your library to keep abreast of social history for conditions of the times, the social structure, what laws existed and what penalties for breaking them, who was able to vote, what epidemics occurred or what slumps in what trades, what emigration was taking place, what immigrants were entering the country, what offences risked transportation, how much (or how little) the ordinary man moved about, the coming of railways, class distinction, changes in the nature of trades – all can help you feel your way to the next step backwards. For instance, it may explain why a wealthy man suddenly died penniless or why another was called a colourman when you had seen him referred to as a druggist.

Many libraries are also the home of the local history society and at worst will have a local interest section, be it ever so small. The librarian in charge of this will be keen to help you and some places have commendable catalogues of their collections of books, manuscripts, maps, newspaper cuttings and maybe rate books (see Chapter Nine).

One of the finest genealogical aids is the directory of a county, town or rural area. It is essential to remember they were compiled in the year preceding their date. Like rate books, these are used to see when an address was first occupied by a given family, to see when a street was built up, to discover a man's occupation if his residence is known and vice versa, to gauge when a man retired or died, to judge the tone of the district, and many other things.

The first directory was one for London published in 1671. Originally they listed only traders, gentry and local officials, but later came to include private residents. They matured into dividing their entries into court lists (i.e. inhabitants, alphabetically), trades, and occupants street by street, with a preliminary description of the locality and a résumé of facilities for worship, carting, the mails, market, stagecoaches and later railways, and a variety of other items.

Many large towns had their own directories from about 1775, while smaller places were catered for only at intervals and might have been lumped together with other areas. Take care with house numbers, which often changed in Victorian times, as did street names. Thus if two addresses are given for your family in census returns ten years apart it may nevertheless have remained in the same spot. Watch to see where the nearest corner occurs and ensure you look in a directory at the correct side of the street each time.

Keep a record of books read and number them. When taking notes add your book number at the end for later reference. Decidedly you do not want to read the same book twice, since one will surely lead to another and you can never hope to read everything! Your research is one long chain anyway: a directory perhaps leads to a will, so back to the PRO, which points to another parish register, so back to the church, which indicates a different trade, so back to the library, which passes you to a livery company . . .

The most famous and by far the best library in the world

is that of the British Museum, which since 1973 has been embraced by the British Library, but even the most modest little branch of the library system is invaluable. Through it hundreds of men and women offer you the fruits of their own labours and smooth your path in so doing. If you need a certain book, your local library will be able either to hand it over from its own shelves or to get it for you through the British Library, which includes the National Central Library nationwide system of loans. It has about 1,750,000 books and 39,000 current periodicals in its own stock and can draw on many millions more. Remember though that the printed word is only as accurate as its transcriber or printer or both.

BRITISH LIBRARY

To use this library you need a reader's ticket, for which apply in writing. Give your full name and permanent address, and state your intention to carry out personal genealogical research. You need a written recommendation from someone in a recognized position, such as a doctor, clergyman or schoolteacher. In return you will be sent, with your ticket, pamphlets on procedure and facilities, which include photocopying services. Virtually every non-fiction book printed in Britain since the 1750s is there, with every published work since 1842, and thousands besides.

For Reading Room and Map Room you can reserve records by postal application to the Superintendent – well worthwhile, as otherwise you can wait for hours. However, even a protracted wait can be of no avail, for without a seat (and they are often at a premium) you will not be handed anything at all. Nor will books be left at your reserved place unless you are there to be held responsible for them.

The Reading Room itself is rather awesome, but the staff are knowledgeable and co-operative and the plan provided to each reader is a good guide to the arrangement of those books on open shelves for you to help yourself. Just remember to keep an eye on the delivery trolley nearing your seat!

Many documents in the vast collection will be beyond your understanding without expert help, but then these are mostly of too early a date to be required by a beginner. Gathered together in this place are charters, plans, manuscripts, returns, heralds' visitations and many other irreplaceable treasures. Lending their weight are such aids as copies up to 1800 of *The Times* (formerly *Daily Universal Register*) and *London Gazette* (formerly *Oxford Gazette*).

NEWSPAPER LIBRARY

This is also under the auspices of the BL. With very extensive collections going back many years, it is covered by the same reader's ticket as the BL itself. Telephone or write first to make sure the paper you want is available, as there were heavy war losses. Although not so accessible as the library itself, it is close to Colindale station on London underground's Northern Line. The atmosphere is much less formal, but the same restrictions apply.

Newspapers were born early in the seventeenth century, since when they have variously merged, died, been re-born, changed their titles, expanded and shrunk, not to mention having supported or decried a variety of social causes and political parties, mirroring the opinions of their particular readerships. Of course, the list of newspapers is far too massive to quote here. Although literacy was so confined in the eighteenth century a veritable host of papers appeared and flourished in London and to a lesser extent in provincial cities, the *Norwich Post* being proudly born in 1701.

The Times is indexed, praise be! But if you do not know the date needed, a search in newspapers can quench all but the brightest flames of resolve, for it is frustrating, exhausting and eye-straining to work through column after column and page after page in an age when presentation was less expert than today. See if you can enlist help from the present office of your chosen paper (remembering mergers, etc.) or the area reference library, which often has a collection. I have found librarians mostly almost embarrassingly helpful. Or try the CRO. Do not despise advertisements, which may have publicized an ancestor's trade or offered his factory for auction.

Below is an example of a well-known newspaper's evolution:

> *Leedes Intelligencer* 1754–65 became
> *Leeds Intelligencer* 1765–1809 became
> *Wright's Leeds Intelligencer* 1809–18 became
> *Leeds Intelligencer & Yorkshire General Advertiser* 1819–66 became
> *Yorkshire Post & Leeds Intelligencer* 1866–83 became
> *Yorkshire Post* 1883–1939 became
> *Yorkshire Post & Leeds Mercury* 1939–

The great thing about newspapers is that they provide immediate contemporary reports on every aspect of life – crime, elections, trade, land deals, social events and so on. If the paper covers a port there is news of ships and cargoes.

A general aid to choice of newspapers, especially if you wish to consult their own archives or perhaps place an inquiry in them, is the *Newspaper Press Directory* (in most libraries). This gives circulation area, establishment date and brief description.

GUILDHALL, LONDON

Guildhalls in general are treasure houses for genealogists, though not many offer library facilities at all, let alone any comparable to those of London's Guildhall, which is a very fine centre indeed. With Victorians it became almost fashionable to take an interest in genealogy and local history. As a result a great many small societies were founded, and the publications which resulted are something you cannot afford to ignore at Guildhall.

Indeed from the mid-eighteenth century there was a healthy demand for the recording of genealogical data, though perhaps more along the lines of social gossip, which resulted in such as the *Gentleman's Magazine* (1731–1907). This can be consulted easily thanks to its index, and is a good source for births, marriages and deaths of the gentry, professional men and tradesmen. Others in like mould include *Notes & Queries*,

London Magazine, *Monthly Magazine*, *Scots Magazine* and *Annual Register*.

Incidentally the Museum of London (incorporating the Guildhall Museum) houses various mementoes of City (i.e. the square mile) civic life and may be worthwhile to visit.

Guildhall Library holds the vast majority of London's guild records, dating from around the mid-fifteenth century to the mid-eighteenth (later dates being covered by records still held by the many livery companies themselves). Guildhall also has a fine collection of maps, as well as prints, drawings, manuscripts and printed books. The index cards show the tremendous range, including probate records and poll books. (See Chapter Eleven.)

Despite the emphasis of all its contents naturally being on the capital much of its collection covers the entire country. There, also, is a marvellous collection of nationwide directories, together with a number of periodical files of immense help. Law reports extend from the seventeenth century to modern times. For the history of a trade or craft you cannot do better than go to Guildhall.

The staff must be nearly unrivalled in their knowledge and excellent accommodation is provided for study, there being a need to be in your seat to receive requested records, as has to be the case where irreplaceable collections are guarded. Just as rightly, you may study only on the premises. Many books are on open shelves, and the now usual photographic facilities are available.

Indexing is divided into authors, London and general. However, perhaps the work you want is not listed and then it is best to approach the inquiry desk, because it just may be at Guildhall nonetheless.

THE SOCIETY OF GENEALOGISTS

The library of this body is of immense value, especially as you need not be a member, although membership is well worthwhile. The society's objects, to use its own words, are 'to promote and to encourage the study of genealogy, topography and heraldry'. It has a first-class library on these topics, growing constantly, and offers a loan system in many, though understandably not all, cases. Unfortunately the rate of lost books through non-return is high.

Items available include the country's largest collection (over 4,000) of parish-register copies, with countless other reference works, documents and indexes relating not only to the obvious items, such as poll books and local histories, but also to many other aspects of life. One of its mainstays is its card index of three million references to families and places, another being a marriage index filling hundreds of volumes embracing somewhere between six and seven million names. The society additionally publishes its own booklets and the quarterly *Genealogists Magazine*, in which one may advertise queries and see where to contact some professional researchers.

Limited research can be undertaken by the society on behalf of members and non-members, the latter being able to use the library for reasonable fees. Monthly during the winter, meetings are held about general and specific research, when members can listen to experts or seek others with similar aims, and there is a catalogue of members' interests.

The society's resources are very large, and mention should be made of the index slips to the calendars of PCC wills and admons from 1750 to 1800, as this is a difficult period when any information you can get is useful. There are also several hundred microfilms taken by the Salt Lake City Genealogical Society of indexes to Scottish births, marriages and deaths 1855–1920, including an alphabetical list by counties, plus the registers themselves for 1855, as well as a fair number of Irish will calendars and marriage licences, an apprenticeship index 1710–74, and Boyd's marriage index 1538–1837.

DR WILLIAMS'S LIBRARY

Mentioned in Chapter Four, it houses the Nonconformist registry.

CROS

All have libraries mainly on their own area, including the relevant volumes of the valuable *Victoria County History*.

There are sure to be maps, maybe photographs and usually something to help with local dialects. (See Chapter Seven.)

BODLEIAN LIBRARY

This is possibly the greatest rival to the BL. It contains virtually every book published in Britain since 1610, as well as many other archives and documents. Anyone with forebears who were at Oxford University should certainly consult it.

LAMBETH PALACE LIBRARY

This holds records of the Vicar-General of the Archbishop of Canterbury, the Faculty Office and others. Included are the parish registers of the Diocese of Canterbury and some peculiars, as well as certain registers for British subjects in Shanghai, Basra, Baghdad, Khartoum and Malta. The Faculty Office records cover marriage allegations and the issuing of marriage licences. At Lambeth, too, are a number of wills and the records of the Court of Arches, which dealt mainly with disputes over marriages and wills.

CAMBRIDGE UNIVERSITY LIBRARY

Akin to the Bodleian above, it naturally holds full records of Cambridge University students.

Besides those specifically mentioned there are a great many specialist libraries. Then there are private collections, often safekeeping anything from little known or needed papers to archives of national importance, while many towns and cities have excellent local collections, among them Birmingham, Exeter, Hull, Sheffield, Wakefield, Wigan and York, to list but a few. All universities have first-class registers and it would be invidious to mention any in particular, except perhaps Oxford and Cambridge.

Died

Nov 18th 1854

William Hall aged 39

Newcastle upon Tyne

Died
August 9th James Francis Hall

Aged 12½ years

Kingston upon Hull

1856

Elizabeth Ann Hall
Died June 1st 1876.   Aged 6? years

Caroline Hall wife of Charles Died July 7th 1877
aged 23 years

Burnell Brown Hall son Wm & M Hall
at Sanatorium Died Dec 7th 9.4 p.m 1899
(nee Brown) Born Apl 1852

Mary Hannah Spencer Hall wife of
William Burnell Dickon Hall died Feb 6 1923
+ an.

William Burnell Dickon Hall
Who passed away June 16th
about 9-45 P.M.
ngston upon Hull.   1927.

In his 85th year.

In Jesus Keeping.

Family bible

GIVEN AT THE GENERAL REGISTER OFFICE,
SOMERSET HOUSE, LONDON

Application Number..........

REGISTRATION DISTRICT

18 50   BIRTH in the Sub-district of _____ in the County of _____

Columns:— 1	2	3	4	5	6	7	8	9	10*
No.	When and where born	Name, if any	Sex	Name and surname of father	Name, surname and maiden surname of mother	Occupation of father	Signature, description and residence of informant	When registered	Signature of registrar	Name entered after registration

CERTIFIED to be a true copy of an entry in the certified copy of a Register of Births in the District above mentioned.
Given at the GENERAL REGISTER OFFICE, SOMERSET HOUSE, LONDON, under the Seal of the said Office, the _____ day of _____ 19___.

*See note overleaf

BX 813662

This certificate is issued in pursuance of the Births and Deaths Registration Act 1953. Section 34 provides that any certified copy of an entry purporting to be sealed or stamped with the seal of the General Register Office shall be received as evidence of the birth or death to which it relates without any further or other proof of the entry, and no certified copy purporting to have been given in the said Office shall be of any force or effect unless it is sealed or stamped as aforesaid.

CAUTION—Any person who (1) falsifies any of the particulars on this certificate, or (2) uses a falsified certificate as true, knowing it to be false, is liable to prosecution.

Form A502M (S.321/24)   Dd. 78531   100,000   10/70   Hw.—RE-30

Birth certificate

Given at the GENERAL REGISTER OFFICE, SOMERSET HOUSE, LONDON

Application Number. 535141

Registration District DURHAM

1855 . Marriage solemnized at **The Parish Church** in the Parish of **St. Giles, Durham** in the **County of Durham**

No.	When married	Name and surname	Age	Condition	Rank or profession	Residence at the time of marriage	Father's name and surname	Rank or profession of father
319	January 21st	William Hall	38	Bachelor	Timber Merchant	Gilesgate	William Hall	Farmer
		Mary Ann Stamp	37	Widow	—	Gilesgate	William Hall	Grocer

Married in the **Parish Church** according to the **Rites and Ceremonies** of the **Established Church by Licence by me** James J. Cundill

This marriage was solemnized between us, { William Hall / Mary Ann Stamp } in the presence of us, { Francis Wright Hall / Isabella Hay Wilson }

CERTIFIED to be a true copy of an entry in the certified copy of a Register of Marriages in the District above mentioned.

Given at the GENERAL REGISTER OFFICE, SOMERSET HOUSE, LONDON, under the Seal of the said Office, the 8th day of September 19 67.

MA 822497

Marriage certificate

CERTIFIED COPY OF AN ENTRY OF DEATH

The statutory fee for this certificate is 3s. 9d.
Where a search is necessary to find the entry,
a search fee is payable in addition.

Given at the GENERAL REGISTER OFFICE,
SOMERSET HOUSE, LONDON.

Application Number 6269

REGISTRATION DISTRICT   Plympton St. Mary.

1852. DEATH in the Sub-district of   Yealmpton   In the County of Devon

No.	When and where died	Name and surname	Sex	Age	Occupation	Cause of death	Signature, description, and residence of informant	When registered	Signature of registrar
445	Twenty fourth February 1852 Wyant Button Plymstock	William Rantliff	Male	61 years	Ship Builder	Inflamation of the Stomach (Gastritis) Certified 14 days	x the mark of Mary Newport Present at the Death Town Chapel Plymstock	Twenty sixth February 1852	William Pearse Registrar

CERTIFIED to be a true copy of an entry in the certified copy of a Register of Deaths in the District above mentioned.

Given at the GENERAL REGISTER OFFICE, SOMERSET HOUSE, LONDON, under the Seal of the said Office, the 2nd day of September 19 ..

DA 521079

This certificate is issued in pursuance of the Births and Deaths Registration Act, 1953. Section 34 provides that any certified copy of an entry purporting to be sealed or stamped with the seal of the General Register Office shall be received as evidence of the birth or death to which it relates without any further or other proof of the entry, and no certified copy purporting to be given in the said Office shall be of any force or effect unless it is sealed or stamped as aforesaid.

CAUTION.—Any person who (1) falsifies any of the particulars on this certificate, or (2) uses a falsified certificate as true, knowing it to be false, is liable to prosecution.

Form A504   Dd.144681 J2M 12/63 Rev—RL-JR

Death certificate

WALES

The National Library of Wales – apart from being the depository for Welsh probate papers dated before 1858 and diocesan records – has manorial, tithe and legal archives stretching back to 1536, as well as a very extensive range of printed books and manuscripts. Some catalogues have been printed. Readers' tickets are needed.

The National Museum of Wales can yield much which is useful; and to study reconstructed scenes from the past visit the Welsh Folk Museum.

SCOTLAND

If you have Scottish ancestors then go to the National Library of Scotland. Its collections are very large and unrivalled in its field. This library operates similarly to the BL, so if you need to study in peace and relative leisure at home then approach your local library for the loan facilities of the Scottish Central Library, with its own 40,000 books and many more on call.

IRELAND

Irish sources are in many ways unique, inasmuch as after Ireland was at last wholly under English authority in 1603, it was divided again by the setting up in 1920 of a separate government for Northern Ireland. Dublin is still the centre for many archives concerning the whole island, and perhaps the best library is the National Library of Ireland.

However, Northern Ireland is well served by the Belfast PRO, which issues a steady stream of first-class record publications. You are recommended to apply for the PRO lists, which cover a very wide range. Invaluable work is also done by the Ulster-Scot Historical Society, whose books can be borrowed through public libraries.

MAPS

Maps may depict anything from one field to the whole of the British Isles. They vary in purpose from showing roads,

parishes, agricultural holdings or development, general topography, defences, and so on *ad infinitum*. Genealogists find
them valuable to see the spread of railways, canal development, land enclosures, mill locations, former afforestation,
and a hundred other items of interest which assist in assess-
ing development of trade, ease of travel, mine workings,
growth of geologically related crafts, periodic importance of
ports or political affiliation.

Maps have been produced from time immemorial to a
greater or lesser degree of accuracy. Some of the finest are
those of John Speed for England and Wales dated 1611, but
being of counties these are aesthetic rather than helpful,
though they do depict certain features. Others accompany
manorial, enclosure and tithe records (see Chapter Ten).

It is often worthwhile arming yourself with maps published by the Institute of Heraldic and Genealogical Studies.
These cover England and Wales and show parochial boundaries, dates of commencement of registers and in addition
probate jurisdictions, which are all-important regarding wills.
Each English map covers a county, except for Yorkshire
which is divided into the three now-vanished Ridings and
except for the City of London, which is overprinted with
streets. The Welsh maps are of North Wales (Anglesey,
Caernarfon, Denbigh and Flint), Central Wales (Merioneth,
Montgomery, Cardigan and Radnor) and South Wales (Pem-
broke, Carmarthen, Brecon and Glamorgan) – old counties.
Very soon now the institute will also offer a handy historical
map of bishops' sees and archdeaconries, showing modern
county boundaries.

In England and Wales, Ordnance Survey maps cover almost any scale up to 10½ ft:1 mile, which even shows lamp
posts, horse troughs and bay windows. It goes without say-
ing that they are of great assistance in pinpointing, say, a
mill or a manor house and are of considerable general
interest. Local OS sections of 6 in.:1 mile are at most public
reference libraries, as well as at CROs. They are variously
dated, but Lancashire and Yorkshire first had this scale between 1840 and 1854. The 25 in.:1 mile are dated 1853–93,

then 1891–1907, then 1906–22, since editions are drawn laboriously over a long period. 1 in.:1 mile exist also from 1805 to 1873, beginning with the South East, though Kent in fact is dated 1801.

Large-scale OS plans (i.e. up to $10\frac{1}{2}$ ft:1 mile) were produced between 1843 and 1894 for most towns, with 50 in.:1 mile from 1911. All major towns were mapped in large scale again between 1943 and 1967, while a new series is being prepared at the present time. By government order in fact, official cartography appeared from around 1794.

CROs naturally hold extensive collections of maps and plans. OS has supplied maps catering for many varied uses and also published reference books, among which is a gazetteer. You will find useful Lewis's *Topographical Dictionary of England*, which gives an account of every place of any small importance.

For Scotland the first fairly large-scale mapping is dated 1747–55, at a scale of 1 in.:1,000 yd. Counting a somewhat false start, Scotland was drawn in various editions by OS from the first half of the nineteenth century.

Ireland's OS maps begin in 1824 and are best studied through Andrews's *Ireland in Maps*.

Deeds of title also incorporate maps from the start of the nineteenth century, some of which are with business, ecclesiastical, guild and private archives. These are often a visual delight and very informative. If your interest centres round a church or vicarage you can apply in writing to the Church Commissioners for permission to examine maps in their care. In reading local histories you are bound to come across maps, too, which invariably offer convenient and illuminating insight into development and sometimes actual planning of towns. (See also Chapter Four.)

A copy of an early eighteenth-century map is illustrated. From it can be seen quite clearly not only who owned the fields and gardens along Mile End Road in east London, but how many acres, roods and poles these plots comprised and their variation in both size and shape. Incidentally there is abundant use of I for J and the old-fashioned long s, e.g.

Johnson and Pesthouse. Ancient footpaths appear. Note the presence of captains' names, almost certainly because of proximity to the river – although they could be army officers and not naval.

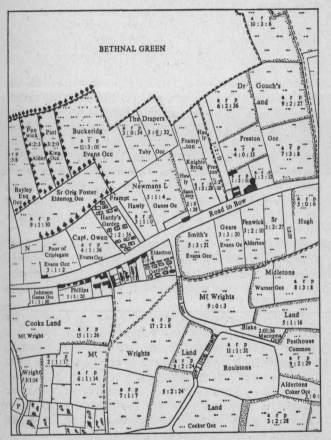

Fig. 8   A copy of Gascoyne's 'Map of the Hamlet of Mile End Old Town', 1703

CHAPTER SEVEN

RECORD SOCIETIES AND OFFICES

NATIONAL

There is no other record repository to compare with the PRO: excellent though others are, the PRO holds the cream, particularly of national archives.

The London PRO national records range from the Norman Conquest onwards, numbering many millions and including such gems as Domesday Book, the Gunpowder Plot papers and Battle of Trafalgar logbooks. Everything is not available for inspection for varying security reasons – some being withheld for thirty years, others for a hundred, etc. On the other hand, those on display in the museum are open to all without ticket formalities.

Unfortunately there is no general index, but a great time-saver at most libraries is HMSO's *Guide to the Public Record Office* (with supplements) and PRO staff are expert and helpful. For some items undoubtedly professional assistance is essential.

The collections are safeguarded at two repositories, for instance census returns and wills at Chancery Lane, but military and tithe redemption records at Kew, so establish beforehand which office you need. When applying for your ticket also request the abundant guiding leaflets. Photographic and photostat facilities are available at reasonable charges, as are microfilm copies. Facilities have now been cancelled for documents to be brought on request from one PRO office to another. (See also Chapter Three.)

For Wales the repository is the National Library of Wales; for Scotland the Scottish Record Office; Northern Ireland and Eire each have a Public Record Office.

REGIONAL

Of recent years county record offices have been accorded much greater respect and status, with increased numbers of private individuals, business enterprises and official bodies acknowledging them as the first places to consult about historical records. Staffed by trained specialists equipped with efficient scientific means of repairing and preserving, these offices are gradually safeguarding the nation's historical records wealth.

There is a certain case against collecting irreplaceable and unique items together, emphasized by tragic wartime losses at Exeter. Nonetheless the genealogist and his research brothers bless the day counties and large towns began setting up these depositories, where loving care is lavished on archives to save them from mould, vermin, damp, mutilation, loss and general ravages of time. Dedicated experts – grossly over-burdened and thus more than worthy of courtesy and consideration – compile specialist volumes by the bookcaseful and still manage to devote their limited time to researchers' specific queries, on the principle of helping them to help themselves.

Some idea of the workload can be given by quoting Essex County Record Office as having had 5,722 personal visits and 1,817 postal or telephone inquiries in one year, with currently some 40 publications in print. The majority of CROs publish reports on their collections. However, despite these offices pertaining theoretically to the historical (i.e. pre-1974) counties, records are often in unexpected repositories and may need considerable tracing. For example, a family may have held land in several counties. CROs can usually advise.

The effects of the 1974 local government reorganization are as yet incomplete. However, present collections will probably be kept as previously, and county changes observed only for new acquisitions. The main archive offices (some awaiting new titles) are listed on page 123 under the new areas, itemizing the old for genealogists, who will ideally be equipped with a map of former and present boundaries.

Like the PRO, CROs (a term used for convenience to cover towns, too) are mentioned continually under specific headings. Many also have complementary local history libraries.

An archivist cannot be expected to entertain (and should not be exasperated by) requests for lengthy searches. However, if you are specific he will comply, though regrettably the odd one may not answer written queries. Let us give him the benefit of the doubt that this is unintentional, if galling.

There is nothing to rival CROs for local data. True, sometimes documents are with the 'wrong' archivist, but usually because there is some connection (e.g. land ownership) with his area. Gradually everything is being sorted and cross-referenced, and the exhaustive items covered are indexed individually. Visiting a CRO will certainly yield something of benefit to you.

DIOCESAN

Diocesan record offices are mostly incorporated in CROs, to which you should direct your inquiries. Specifically for probate records, see Chapter Five.

Remember that some parishes are peculiars and therefore are not under a bishop's jurisdiction: approach the CRO for advice, because most often peculiars' records have been deposited there. Sadly, peculiars' independence has frequently resulted in a careless or ailing incumbent not having safeguarded his records against loss, which can be disastrous particularly if (in excess of his authority) he issued marriage licences.

Tithe awards are usually among diocesan records, with maps and apportionments describing plots of land and naming owners or occupiers. Apart from obvious archives connected with clergy there are also records of church courts dealing with religious offences, such as fornication or non-observance of the Sabbath Day, together with misdemeanours more suited to trial and punishment by lay courts. Bishops were responsible for licensing parish clerks, surgeons, school-masters and the like, as well as marriages. They also held transcripts of parish registers, in theory at least.

Wales

Apply for diocesan records to the National Library of Wales, remembering that nonconformity is widespread in the principality.

Scotland

Apply initially to the Scottish Genealogical Society.

Northern Ireland

For Church of Ireland, Roman Catholic or Presbyterian records apply to the Ulster-Scot Historical Society. All these churches have substantial followings.

Eire

Seek direction from the Irish Genealogical Research Society.

MISCELLANEOUS RECORD OFFICES AND SOCIETIES

For the Society of Genealogists see Chapter Six.

It has already been stated that in general guildhalls hold many useful items, and that London's is probably the best. Under its umbrella is the Corporation of London Record Office (relating to the City only), which has archives ranging from William the Conqueror. Although in general they are of greater interest to the historian than the genealogist, there are also details of freemen and apprentices from modern times back to about 1540. A guide has been published.

Guildhalls may offer wills, deeds, crime dossiers or taxation information for whole households, and have always been closely associated with local trade and guilds. In ports there will certainly be papers relevant to ships, boats and maybe the Navy. If your interest is transport try the British Transport Historical Records Office collection.

One source which might be overlooked, is the Royal Humane Society, founded 1774. If you have an ancestor who won the society's medals for saving life then you can boost your pride with details, and of course the incident may have been reported in a home or overseas newspaper.

CHAPTER EIGHT

EARNING A LIVING

There is much to be said for working out the probable vagaries of a man's life from the way he earned his daily bread, using common sense and imagination. For example, if you know he was a tradesman this will suggest his own and his staff's apprenticeships, maybe title deeds, almost certainly a will, quite likely at least rudimentary education, very possibly a vote (with its pre-1872 non-secret political bias), perhaps horse ownership, and so on. All this can fertilize your tree. Not just intriguing in its own right, it also points to further branches: an apprenticeship indenture might give the name of a boy's father, for instance.

Working-class life was aggravated by periodic trade slumps when unemployment was rife and starvation familiar, and when work did exist payment was pitifully low. Added hazards were threatened disability through disease or employers' malpractices, plus family destitution and appearance in workhouse records.

Fast population increase caused mid-eighteenth-century industry to grow. Among the effects were the killing of 'cottage industries', for which families toiled at home, as well as considerable movement of rural labour to towns and a more restrictive life, with probably more child workers than ever previously known. Workers (without the right to strike) attempted to unite spasmodically but only to the extent of the odd riotous assembly, until general exploitation and fear of widespread unemployment through machinery inventions gave rise to the Luddite movement in 1811. Adherents who not only destroyed machinery, but also demanded fair pay, were met by a harsh government with public whipping and even hanging, duly recorded in legal and prison documents. Many tradesmen were bankrupted around 1800 and finished in debtors' prisons. In 1785 a shop duty had been introduced, while at times licences were necessary to sell many commodities. Try your CRO for these.

In 1797, banknotes – though not by any means novel – were issued by many banking houses, the failure of a number of which caused hundreds of their customers to be declared bankrupt, particularly in market towns.

Many businessmen do not fit into any of the categories below but possibly feature in printed histories of commercial companies, charitable or other institutions, banks or councils. A vast number exist, many of them illustrated. There are also records of board or shareholders' meetings which could mention or maybe quote your man, as well as newspaper, trade-magazine or house-journal articles, but there has been a flood of mergers and takeovers (not merely recently), a good example being that of banks.

The PRO London contains certain documentation on patents, designs and trade marks, some dating back to 1617.

SEAFARING

This includes all types of mariners, and therefore refers to the Royal Navy, what is now the Merchant Navy and fishing fleets, as well as shipowners.

Your introduction to this sphere may well be through GRO certificates as mentioned in Chapter Two. The easiest step then to find an officer is to search the Navy Lists at the PRO or BL, by which it is normally fairly easy to piece together his age, details of death and whole career at sea or ashore.

For merchant officers and other ranks in all forms of fleet your best source is the PRO London. However, Royal Navy officers' data (including marriage details 1806–1902) are there, too. Among these are records of campaign medals – often issued late – prisoners-of-war, musters, pay for both mariners and dockyard staff, discharges, casualties, men who fell sick and pensions for wounded, widows and orphans. Description books, musters and logbooks reveal name, duties, rank, age, birthplace, height, complexion, distinguishing features (for example, a missing eye or finger, scar, large mole) and even the colour of eyes. Certificates for all grades are fairly complete from 1691 to the early twentieth century.

Logs are fascinating in themselves, and can shed much light on bare facts if a man caught the pox or died falling from the rigging. They range from 1669 to currently 1920. Again, though incidentally, there is information concerning convicts being transported 1817–53 (with a 20 per cent death rate) and emigrants 1815–53 who were given some- times not much better passage.

The Merchant Navy in general is best chronicled by the formerly Cardiff-based Registrar General of Shipping & Seamen records, under the old Board of Trade. They parti- ally encompass earlier times, but so far as crewmen are concerned mainly date from 1835 only, because that is when the law first decreed seamen must be registered with details of service. Fortunately there is an alphabetical index. Sea- going tickets were introduced in 1844 and incorporated quite extensive details, but were abolished in 1854. Registration itself did not cease until 1856, and of course crew lists con- tinue to supply basic needs.

Masters and mates were encouraged from 1845 to pass examinations which became compulsory in 1850, their sep- arate registers being divided into competency, service, foreign trade, home trade and specifically foreign service on steam- ships. They cover ships relative to individuals' seagoing careers and many genealogical details, including injuries, retirements and deaths, and are indexed.

Engineers' certificates and index date from 1862, but not till 1883 were skippers and mates of fishing boats drawn into the system. They, too, have an index. Masters, mates and engineers who passed Colonial examinations have their own registers, but for index purposes are included with engineers in general. Apprentices feature in separate lists and are indexed also.

Further documents available deal with wages and effects of deceased seamen, indexed by names of both men and ships, personnel of the Royal Naval Reserve instituted in 1859 and composed of seamen and fishermen, and disciplinary measures taken. Seamen's wills at the PRO date roughly from 1786 to 1880.

As far as muster rolls are concerned, from 1747 ship-owners were obliged to list their crewmen. Thus the PRO has names of individuals and their ships, together with residences and recruitment dates. It is too bad that so many musters have been lost before 1800, but there are some earlier for Dartmouth, Liverpool and Plymouth and those for North and South Shields survive from 1747. There is little point in consulting them after 1835, when modern crew lists began, with a written personal agreement for each seaman on board either a foreign-going UK-owned ship, a fishing vessel or a coaster. Agreements eventually were lodged with the Regi-strar General of Shipping & Seamen, and can be found with musters, though only a tenth have been preserved after 1860 by the PRO, which can advise on the whereabouts of the remainder. In any case it might be more worthwhile to con-sult ships' census returns from 1861.

Agreements and crew lists for fishing vessels under eighty-ton burden were introduced as late as 1883 – again unluckily only a tenth being at the PRO – while there is a specialist class for certain ships with a particular claim to fame.

The PRO Board of Trade category applies to classes of records for merchant shipping and the above-mentioned Royal Naval Reserve documents. Nowadays all the UK armed forces are absorbed within the Ministry of Defence but previously were autonomous, the RN being controlled by the Admiralty – whose passing surely saddens any his-torian. It is in Admiralty archives that the PRO stores all RN papers from the mid-seventeenth century, with dates earlier than 1660 among domestic State papers in Exchequer records.

To take a somewhat short cut to check on promotions, casualties and awards use the *London Gazette* files at the BL or Guildhall, London.

The National Maritime Museum has an understandable prejudice towards the famous, but also presents a wealth of detail regarding all classes of vessels and their appurtenances.

In tracing someone at sea you will find it helpful to discover something of their ships, as indeed also if your ancestor was a shipowner or shipbuilder. A ticket is necessary to use the Reading Room.

With an idea of place and date of interest you can use such newspapers as *Lloyd's List* (established 1734) or *Journal of Commerce* (established 1825), the latter being of Liverpool but covering the whole country. Knowing perhaps from a marriage certificate that a seaman was in, say, Liverpool on a given date you can see what ships were in that port then and compile a short list of vessels for him.

As to ships themselves, you can obtain technical details from Lloyd's Register of Shipping, or by personal examination of *Lloyd's Register* or the *Mercantile Navy List*, both at the PRO, if the appropriate date is 1760 or later. No promises can be made, but for the mid-nineteenth century you could find, for example: year and port of registration; name of master (perhaps different in subsequent years); name of owner; material; type or rig; net tonnage; place and date of building; length, breadth and depth; type of trade; when last registered.

The Merchant Shipping Act 1786 obliged British ship-owners to register all decked vessels of more than fifteen tons, whether built at home or abroad – which exempted almost nothing, so you can refer to Customs records (from 1786 for London but otherwise from 1814 only, owing to fire losses) at the PRO London. They give after 1825 such additional titbits as owners' occupations and addresses, name and employment of surveying officer, and technical details including presence of galley or figurehead. It is also stated if the ship was captured as a prize. After 1854 every ship had an official registration number, as opposed to port number.

Marking fishing-boats' hulls with official letters and numbers became law in 1894. Thus their registration dates and details from then are in the PRO. Registration of barges and other craft over thirteen tons on rivers, canals and lakes became compulsory in 1795. Wooden ships were still being built in the 1860s, steam power and iron having been adopted in the 1840s and steel in the 1850s. In the mid-nineteenth century most commercial ships voyaging worldwide were of only 500 tons or less. Deepsea trades saw barques, barquentines, brigs and brigantines, while shortsea and coastal trips were served by smacks, ketches and schooners. Browsing among PRO naval papers is often hazardous, as their fascination can divert. One has only to think of the *Bounty* and the repercussions of that famous mutiny to imagine the risks to the researcher!

Sailors have hailed from all social classes, but most ordinary crewmen in past centuries were humble folk, often enlisting because of trouble with the law or the ladies. Conditions on board were unattractive, to put it mildly, unless a man was unable to find another livelihood, and pay meagre (about 1670–1797 only 19s a month and unbelievably in arrears). Even officers usually needed a private income, being therefore frequently of the upper or middle class, though there were individuals like Captain Cook who were not.

Quarter Sessions records at CROs sometimes have lists of men on naval service during the Napoleonic Wars. Greenwich Hospital lists naval pensioners 1704–1869, with dates of enrolment and some career details, also at the PRO.

If a nineteenth-century seaman lost his ticket, he was barred from sailing unless he could raise the formidable sum of 13s for another, so he might reappear as a dock labourer or stevedore or something entirely different. Up to 1928 he could join an American merchantman – though not as master, who had by law to be an American citizen after about 1850 – and if you suspect this then contact the General Services Administration, National Archives & Records Service, for crew lists or ships' particulars and movements.

Often overlooked are Trinity House Petitions, now with the Society of Genealogists, being appeals to the Corporation of Trinity House by mariners and their dependants 1780–1854 for financial assistance. They include extremely valuable genealogical details. The Navy Records Society is also helpful. Apply to the PRO also for records of the Royal Marines, instituted as a corps in 1664.

See also Chapter Two – at sea, and overseas.

MILITARY

This section covers not only soldiers but also militiamen, who were the precursors of Terriers – Territorial Army members, not to be confused with terriers, the recorded legal rights to some form of property, usually in connection with churches and frequently respecting land, generally dated after 1600.

An army officer in your family was probably an aristocrat of some kind, but a private would have been of low class. Like sailors, the 'common soldier' usually joined for one of four reasons – drink, unemployment, women or the law – for army life was hardly more enticing than the navy and the respectable tended to fight shy of it. Officers on the other hand were often of better family than their naval counterparts. Some bought their commissions, a facility abolished about 1870, and invariably they needed private means because of the poor pay. From 1793 to 1891 a regular private received 1s a day and had to provide his own food and clothing.

Eighteenth-century soldiers were often the sons of farmers, labourers, craftsmen, shopkeepers and impoverished clergymen, although all social classes were represented by them by the following century. Officers were esquires if they were captains or above, as thereby they enjoyed Crown commissions, and captains appointed their own subalterns.

With the army, various wars have to be considered, even though many are not recorded in depth. Wars themselves are often responsible for military evolution, which is important in some ways for a genealogist. As opposed to the old system whereby nobility and gentry somewhat amateurishly led their own men as required, effectively from 1642 England had a regular army – a direct result of Charles I's confrontation with the House of Commons, leading to the Civil War. Their story can be read in Firth and Davies's *The Regimental*

History of Cromwell's Army, with lists of regiments and officers of both armies in Peacock's *The Army List of Round-heads and Cavaliers*. Other wars that may concern you include the American War of Independence (1776–81), involving troops from Canada as well as Britain. The Peninsular War (1803–13) saw the Rifle Brigade's establishment. During the Napoleonic Wars press gangs became most notorious, so that the most unlikely ancestor may have been forced under arms. Militiamen frequently transferred to regular army regiments. It is easy to imagine young men rallying to the colours when invasion threatened from the French shores, just as their descendants did in 1914 and 1940.

Minor wars were waged sporadically on the Indian continent. These and the pressing need to safeguard Britain's eastern trading interests caused many troops to serve there for whole lifetimes. The Crimean War began in 1854 and lasted an almost feverishly hectic eighteen months, followed immediately by hostilities with China and almost simultaneously the Indian Mutiny. In 1861 the four-year American Civil War began, and though it did not involve the British Army, there were important trade repercussions affecting seamen. The next large-scale military confrontation was the Boer or South African War of 1899–1902, succeeded by the two World Wars of 1914–18 and 1939–45.

PRO records of regular soldiers engaged in the Boer War unfortunately were mostly, though not wholly, lost during World War II bombing. However, certain documents survive regarding yeomanry and volunteers, and are in the PRO for the former and London's Guildhall for the latter. There is material available in the PRO for British troops involved in the American War of Independence and with the British army in India, excluding in some instances engineers and gunners. For records concerning the Indian (i.e. Imperial) Army and the East India Company, on the other hand, apply to the Foreign and Commonwealth Office.

Sandhurst Military Academy was founded in 1802, greatly influenced by England's warring with Holland, Spain and France, not to mention involvement with the United States, Ireland, India, Russia, Prussia, Sweden and Denmark. Military police became a permanent army feature only as late as 1855.

By far the best army collections are those of the PRO London, but it cannot be emphasized too strongly that you need to know the regiment, as the records are arranged accordingly. Here are service records of commissioned officers dating from 1660 (Restoration of the Monarchy), though without details of family or birthplace until the very late 1700s. There are widows' pension applications from around 1795, and officers' deaths in the paymaster general's records. Also available are officers on the active list (1829–1919) or retired (1828) on either half or full pay, with their births, marriages and births of children. The PRO offers basic pay lists, muster rolls and discharge certificates, backed up by a host of subsidiary records: description books, with enlistment ages, casualty returns, Chelsea Hospital pension registers, pension registers of the Royal Hospital, Kilmainham, Dublin, all stating birthplaces, and also certificates for discharged pensioners from 1760 (some earlier) and for all discharged men from 1883 – all with various family details. There are also arrest certificates for deserters and bounty certificates for apprehenders, both from around 1720 and part-indexed.

Description books give soldiers' ages, trades, heights, colourings and complexions. Pay lists and muster rolls stretch sparsely from Norman times, and in full from 1760. For modern ones contact the Ministry of Defence for officers or for any rank the various army record offices listed in *Whitaker's*. Muster rolls are arranged by ranks within regiments, and give age, place and date of enlistment, military record, pay, discharge date and any details of wounds or imprisonment. Birthplaces and trades appear for soldiers who became 'non-effective' as distinct from being discharged on pension or dying, and from about 1868 muster rolls include marriages and children. At the end of them are notes on soldiers who had ceased to be included through desertion or death, and these should show birthplaces. Obviously a man found thus should be traceable back through similar lists for his regiment, and his age on enlistment established.

Fairly certainly you will need to inquire how the modern army has merged regiments. To do this study Swinson's *A Register of the Regiments & Corps of the British Army*. This book on origins has an admirable index and excellent cross-references, which allow for identification merely from the nickname of a particular body of soldiers and also reliably indicate what military actions took place and when. It is not infallible, but is a first-class introduction to military affairs prior to reading a regimental history.

I once needed to trace a man named Smith who was said to be a Hull colour-sergeant at Waterloo and previously a prisoner in the Peninsular War – hardly a promising start. Simple research disclosed that the rank of colour-sergeant is peculiar to infantry of the line regiments, including Highlanders. Napoleonic War histories stated that there were twenty-four infantry regiments which fought at Waterloo, of which seven were not in the Peninsular War, leaving a balance of seventeen. One was the Yorkshire Light Infantry and another the 95th Foot or Rifle Brigade, which raised certain battalions in Hull and therefore offered a springboard. PRO muster rolls of the pertinent Rifle Brigade battalions showed seventeen companies in the Peninsular at any one time, and revealed the man fairly easily because there was only one colour-sergeant to each company. Thus the most hopeless case can finish quite successfully.

From the Napoleonic Wars, too, men from all ranks began writing their memoirs.

Among clerk of the peace records, CROs often have lists of payments to militiamen's wives and families during the Napoleonic Wars. Also a 1757 Act called for county lists of all men capable of bearing arms, while from 1799 it was usual to list killed and wounded. A number of militiamen fought against Bonaparte, and whether transferred to a regular regiment or not sometimes qualified for pensions. Militia attestation papers, in addition to birth details, state employers' names 1860–1914. Most local militia and volunteer records are in lieutenancy papers at CROs.

Medal rolls provide certain details (1793–1904) but at times campaign medals have been issued very much in arrears

– as was the Peninsular General Service Medal, distributed 1849. The highest British military award is the Victoria Cross, instituted in 1856.

Whitaker's Almanack lists army record offices where inquiries can be made direct to a regiment, remembering always any reorganization. To learn more since 1914 a visit to the Imperial War Museum would be worthwhile. There is also the official National Army Museum. The Royal Hospital at Chelsea (founded 1682 for old and disabled soldiers) has admission books from 1715. The Society for Army Historical Research or the Military Historical Society should be able to assist, and the *London Gazette* publishes army promotions, casualties and awards – accessible at the BL or London's Guildhall.

ROYAL AIR FORCE

This was born 1918 and was preceded by the Royal Flying Corps. In common with the Navy and Army, RAF promotions, casualties and awards appear in *London Gazette* (BL or Guildhall, London). For general help apply to the Royal Air Force Association or to the Ministry of Defence ARS (RAF).

PROFESSIONS

The legal profession is exceptionally well-documented through records held by universities, inns of court, professional institutions and societies for judges, barristers and solicitors. To a lesser degree, perhaps, the same applies to all members of the medical profession, including dentists and veterinarians – indeed all graduates of universities and colleges, including the clergy and Civil Service. Your library will provide guidance to printed records and of course you may contact the various bodies direct, but mostly the older archives are with CROs.

There are *Law Lists*, individual universities' calendars, *Medical Register*, *Crockford's Clerical Directory* (and its predecessors), *Consulting Engineers' Who's Who*, *Diplomatic*

Service List, *Directory of Directors*, *Royal Institute of British Architects' Directory*, and so on.

About 1870 it became necessary for civil servants to sit competitive examinations, whereas previously they had been admitted to the Civil Service by nomination and patronage. In England and Wales solicitors must pass the Law Society examinations, in Scotland those of the Law Society of Scotland. To be called to the Bar requires successful completion of studies at the Inner Temple, Middle Temple, Lincoln's Inn or Gray's Inn, all in London, or the Faculty of Advocates, Edinburgh. Any should be able to look up particulars of your barrister ancestor for you, and anyway their records are printed.

Graduates in law, theology (Christian and Jewish), medicine and so on are registered at most universities, but remember the earlier the date the fewer the institutions. The oldest college at Oxford was established in 1249 and that at Cambridge in 1284, though both universities were recognized previously. Libraries can produce copies of Foster's *Alumni Oxonienses* or Venn's *Alumni Cantabrigienses* – extensive lists of students at Oxford and Cambridge respectively, giving ages and parentages – but always verify any entries with the universities themselves.

The Society of Genealogists holds the Fawcett Index, which is a large collection of details relating to clergymen and their families, confined to northern England. The clergy were considered low-class between the Reformation and the end of the eighteenth century, when their status rose.

PARLIAMENT

Both Houses of Parliament lodge their records with the House of Lords Record Office. Official printings of proceedings are known as *Hansard* and date from 1803: if an ancestor was a member of Parliament or a peer and you wish to feast on his speeches, questions and answers, he will have been reported verbatim from 1909. The archives in general stretch back much earlier regarding the Lords, but those for the Commons suffered extensive fire losses in 1834.

Local, and to a lesser extent national, newspapers give election background information, and of course libraries have reference books on the various political parties. Conservatives are erstwhile Stuart-supporting Tories, while today's Liberals are yesterday's Whig supporters of the Hanoverian monarchy in Britain from which sprang Queen Victoria.

THEATRE

An excellent (albeit infant) museum is comprised in the Raymond Mander & Joe Mitchenson Theatre Collection. Gradually it is being developed to include as much theatrical biographical data and memorabilia as possible.

TRADE UNIONS

The forerunners of trade unions were eighteenth-century trade clubs, which met in coffee-houses or taverns serving as centres where skilled workmen could be found by masters needing them. Clubs themselves also took on apprentices as they became better organized and ran sickness and burial funds. Some federations of these clubs became trade unions, and developed into national bodies, which implies records.

The first technically legal combinations of workers to form unions were established in 1825. Their records vary so it is rather a case of pot luck if you are relying on them, but look up their addresses in *Whitaker's* and give them a try. Many early unionists were highly skilled, and most trades had their own representative bodies by the twentieth century.

CRAFT AND TRADE GUILDS

Conversely guilds were combinations, born in the twelfth century, of masters with a common trade. By degrees they became extremely well organized, guarding their archives jealously as they vied for status, though none can hope to compare with the great London guilds with their magnificent halls and extensive wealth.

Most London archives are entrusted to Guildhall Library, although modern records naturally remain with surviving guilds or livery companies. Again *Whitaker's* gives addresses. Nowadays they range from air pilots to wheelwrights, number eighty-four with about 10,000 liverymen, and obviously are not all ancient. Provincial records may be with local guildhalls or CROs.

Guild records in both capital and provinces include those of freemen, apprentices and offenders, often providing addresses, scope of business and insight into contemporary trade conditions. Even if you cannot trace what you need in a provincial town you may be assisted by London records, which are in some respects nationwide. Local libraries again prove their worth in providing location of guild offices.

One of the richest London guilds is the Goldsmiths Company. These gentlemen were called upon during the Civil War to finance the government and thus from about 1650 or so gradually evolved as bankers. See also sections on freemen and apprentices.

TRADE DESCRIPTIONS

Occupations often had different connotations from today's and also unfamiliar combinations. Therefore a man may be listed in what appears to be the wrong trade category. Beware of being caught out – you may indeed have traced another individual, or you may have discovered another side to his occupation. A baker, for example, may feature too as grocer, druggist, oilman, colourman or draper. Less surprisingly he may be described as cheese-factor, tea-dealer or even ginger-beer manufacturer! One man may be all of these, even if in business comparatively modestly. Another example is a silk mercer-furrier whose business embraced bonnet-making. A cabinet-maker may appear as upholsterer or chair-maker; a flour-dealer may have been cow-keeper also. Libraries can help by providing the history of a particular trade, or you can appeal to modern trade associations for guidance. Guilds are usually very helpful.

It helps sometimes to discover how different occupations evolved and even when foodstuffs such as spices or coffee were introduced, were scarce or readily available. A tradesman who dealt in a commodity which had hardly reached the Englishman's table must have catered for moneyed customers, have upheld good standards and have had a flourishing business. Pepperers and spicers were the first drugsellers, partly because they also dealt in herbs. Some became grocers, but those who specialized in drugs became apothecaries, who also sold gingerbread because it was considered part-medicinal. In 1815 by virtue of a legal change many were looked upon as medical practitioners. Apothecaries and barber surgeons, being medical men of sorts, often accompanied doctors attending patients. The Pharmaceutical Society of Great Britain was established in 1841.

Our silk-mercer friend started life as a mere silk weaver, so progress has also to be observed in checking status. Other occupations no longer exist; yet others can be confusing such as innholder and innkeeper. The former was licensed to sell liquor but may not in fact have administered the inn himself, while the latter merely dispensed liquor on another's authority. Incidentally taverns, inns, alehouses and hostelries are all distinctive.

POLICE

The 'Peelers' formed the first true police force, instituted by Sir Robert Peel (hence also 'Bobbies') in 1829, and covered only London until spreading further afield. There had been the Bow Street Runners from about 1750, but these were just a few stalwarts employed privately in London. For policemen's records approach the staff controllers of appropriate regional forces.

CHAMBER OF COMMERCE

A multitude of trade associations exists for both employers and employees. All such organizations can be pinpointed through appropriate telephone directories, libraries, councils and newspaper offices, and many circulate to libraries yearbooks incorporating lists of members. Maybe in past editions you will find your ancestor, or at least learn a little of his livelihood. Alternatively you may gather something from the PRO's old Board of Trade records.

In some ways local chambers of commerce are modern guilds, but do not confine themselves to one trade or craft. Although much younger, they can give members' details over the last hundred years or so.

APPRENTICES

The Statute of Artificers 1563 enacted that to practise a craft, every boy and girl had to train for seven years under a master or mistress responsible for them. Such a boy was not free to marry until he was twenty-four or to set up in business or hire himself as journeyman. This marriage ban was later amended to apply during apprenticeship and in time terms varied for particular trades, so read a trade's history or make inquiries through its official modern body – try the telephone directory, *Whitaker's* or your library. Many illegitimate births resulted from apprenticeship forbidding marriage.

In medieval times completion of apprenticeship by boys but not girls, automatically gave them municipal freedom, inherited by their eldest sons, and later by other sons, so it is easy to see how useful apprenticeship records can be apart from helping with dates and trades.

There were different types of apprentice: some were younger sons of gentlemen; some paupers or orphans and placed with craftsmen or merchants by the parish, therefore figuring in churchwardens' accounts which are easily traceable through CROs; some apprenticed officially to their own parents or other relatives. The four inns of court keep good records of legal apprentices.

Apprenticeship age varied also, but usually was from about thirteen to seventeen. In 1710 a tax was placed on indentures and thereafter these (issued by justices of the peace) state the boy's name, that of his father or mother and his master, trade, fee and perhaps residences of father and master. After 1760 they were briefer, and you will not find parish apprentices or those paying less than 1s because they were exempt from tax.

In Elizabethan times the gentry's younger sons were invariably apprenticed to trade or the law if not sent into the Church, the army or diplomacy. This was the norm until George I, when the landed classes began to develop snobbishness over thus 'demeaning' their families. However, many upper-class families had achieved their social position by earlier generations enriching themselves in the subsequently despised field of trade.

Many apprentices were parish liabilities, having been abandoned or orphaned, and, being forced on pain of fine upon unwilling masters, were frequently abused in every way. All apprentices ran this risk of abuse for generations, and most children had begun to earn their keep by the age of four or five. This is not to say that there were no children happily integrated into masters' homes and families.

Because of this tax, the PRO has apprenticeship books 1710–1810, but be wary because the dates refer to when tax was paid and not apprenticeship begun, which may differ by several years. Indexes are divided into masters and apprentices. Previously, proper recording applied only to London (in Guildhall) and a few other towns. However, the Society of Genealogists has Crisp's Bonds, which cover 18,000 names from the sixteenth to the nineteenth centuries and indexed indentures 1641–1888.

From 1712 to roughly 1814 (repeal of Apprentices Act) apprenticeship gradually declined, starting in the wool trade, and by about 1800 periods varied and many apprentices had no legal agreement. The more skilled trades best retained their apprentices, but often with inferior training. About 1835 obligatory apprenticeship ceased and tradesmen no longer had to belong to a company, but of course the system still continues.

Although the seven-year official training was obligatory by law, there were some who set up in trade regardless and were prosecuted – not necessarily resulting in their businesses terminating.

Certain records of parish apprentices are among parish archives held by CROs. Up to the end of the seventeenth century there may have been a register of these children in your area, but only after that were there written contracts. In time forms were produced in which the general conditions read:

> ... The said Apprentice his Master shall faithfully serve, his secrets keep, his lawful commands every where gladly do. He shall do no damage to his said Master nor see to be done of others, but to his Power shall prevent or forthwith give warning to his said Master of the same. He shall not waste the goods of his said Master, nor lend them unlawfully to any. He shall not play at Cards or Dice Tables or any other unlawful Games whereby his said Master may have any loss with his own goods or others during the said Term with Licence of his said Master. He shall neither buy nor sell. He shall not haunt Taverns or Playhouses, nor absent himself from his said Master's service day or night unlawfully. But in all things as a faithfull Apprentice he shall behave himself towards his said Master and all his during the said Term.

Guilds sometimes have accounts showing apprentices' admissions, and for those entering the law or navy see sections on professions and seafaring.

FREEMEN

For records of borough freemen from the mid-sixteenth century contact the town clerk, borough librarian, or perhaps CRO for the area concerned. They show when and how a man qualified for the freedom, which was by patrimony, apprenticeship, purchase, or some service to the borough. Benefits were exemption from various tolls, business protection, the vote, and participation in borough administration, since often freemen were also burgesses. There were often additional local privileges. However, freemen were responsible for providing schools, organizing exports and controlling both prices and quality of goods. They also took an oath of allegiance to the Crown. Overall the honour warranted the respect accorded it.

A freeman was usually styled 'citizen and draper', 'citizen and baker', or whatever. This can be helpful, but try to ensure which calling he followed, because he may have belonged to a particular company only for the honour and privilege and actually have been something quite different. The Municipal Reform Act of 1835 was designed to combat much of the prevalent corruption in local affairs, and one effect was greatly to restrict the bestowing of borough freedom. The Local Government Act 1882 was responsible for freedom becoming even more difficult to achieve, and now it is almost unrecognizable. Many individuals are unaware of their entitlement to it. Any man who has outgrown his minority and whose father was a freeman may boast the honour for himself, as he may if it has missed a generation from father to son.

Freemen's actual registers date from the 1690s. Their names and occupations may also be in guild records, but these often require hard hunting. Almost without exception freemen's bodies have petitioned the Crown or Parliament at some time, and your ancestor's signature could feature here.

The year 1835 saw the first democratically elected borough councils, extended to whole counties or parts of them (excluding county boroughs) in 1888 in place of justices of the peace. Only then was the London County Council (now Greater London Council) founded, the City of London retaining its independent jurisdiction.

Borough freemen and guild freemen were frequently one and the same, so you need to examine both bodies' records to get a complete picture.

FREEMASONS

In a way closely allied with unions and guilds are free-masonry bodies, which have equally good records. Any dates obtainable from this source will help to pinpoint movements. Apart from the certain knowledge that some-one was a freemason, a lodge will not of course disclose any masonic information; but often it can state age, occupa-tion and date of death, as well as period of membership and possibly details of birth also. It can assist in discovering changed residences. Local libraries will advise here, too, or get the appropriate lodge address from the United Grand Lodge of England.

Originating as a craft guild, freemasonry evolved into a philosophical and moral organization with an avowed phil-anthropic aim and gradually spread to the continent and beyond. The Grand Lodge was established in 1717 and be-came suspect (in some quarters condemned, notably by the Catholic Church) because of its semi-political affiliations and somewhat secretive image.

WORKING CHILDREN

Census returns evidence all too often the abuse of Victorian children, but this had been the case long before then. The struggle to survive on low wages and the generally high birthrate (despite high deathrate) had always meant that all hands were needed for plough, loom and to a lesser extent counter, almost without pause. When the ordinary man's off-spring were merely the result of enjoyment, as opposed to completion of a family circle, practical issues were all that mattered. Lucky the lad and lass born into the gentry and bidden at worst to study their books, manners and dress! Their humbler brothers and sisters were miniature men and women, mostly without need even of the ability to sign their names.

The most humble were orphans and foundlings. These be-came parish officers' headaches, so the CRO should have records of parish apprentices foisted on local tradesmen or blatantly thrust out as cheap labour to mills, factories, mines, farms. While obviously there must have been sympathetic, kindly families, a great many households treated these children appallingly. Nevertheless parish children were probably better off as apprentices than those sent into factories or mines.

Even after the 1833 Factory Act children of 12 years or less could still be worked eight hours a day and those aged 13–17 twelve. In 1842 Lord Shaftesbury managed to get through Parliament an Act which forbade employment underground of children under ten. Chimneysweeping by boys was finally banned in 1875 (again to the lasting credit of Shaftesbury).

If unfortunately you need to search among the records of child workers they can be found at CROs and in the poor or parliamentary archives at the PRO – but it will not surprise you to learn that few individual children are traceable. The best (if this is the word) of the general records are reports to Parliament made by a number of zealous, praiseworthy Victorian reformers, though they make harrowing reading. Another general source is Mayhew's *London Labour & the London Poor*.

AGRICULTURE

Farms are so closely linked with landholding that much data will be found in title deeds and wills. These often list occupiers and acreages, sometimes with a note of servants, labourers, sheep, cattle and horses, or with trading details. Deeds set out any tithes due, and the parish chest commonly yields correspondence between incumbent and farmer. Probably the greatest source regarding agriculture is tithe and enclosure recording (Chapters Nine and Ten). The PRO also holds records of landowners who were known Royalist supporters during the Civil War.

It is very unusual not to see the local farming community mentioned in early directories. Corn and cattle prices and suchlike feature in local newspapers, while landowners' and tenants' names appear on field maps. Knowledge can be gained, too, from local land taxation records and legal papers dealing with farmland taken to build railways, roads or canals. Of much earlier date are manorial records.

As a guide, 300 acres constituted a medium-sized farm in 1815, while 500 acres was a large holding. Sixteenth- and seventeenth-century yeomen farmers (freeholders) were for the most part Protestants of good education and long pedigree, and formed the bulk of a large, respected middle class. Many became wealthy thanks to the Napoleonic Wars, although a high proportion were ruined by the subsequent slump. A tenant farmer was described either simply as husbandman or farmer, but husbandmen were often merely labourers.

Gamekeepers' registers date from 1710 and are in quarter sessions archives (probably with the CRO). In the same source are registers of 40s freeholders from 1788 or so.

TRADE TOKENS

At times tradesmen commonly issued their own coinage for convenience, with possibly an inscription starting on the obverse and ending on the reverse. Perhaps also would appear some indication of the trade involved and always mention of the individual's name, maybe with his likeness. It is unlikely that you will have the luck to come across one relating to an ancestor, but not inconceivable that there may be a record of his trade tokens or even an illustration in a local history.

CHAPTER NINE

RATES AND TAXES

Governments have always sought to raise revenue for wars and personal whims. Here are those records of most interest for your research, all of which constitute legal evidence.

RATE BOOKS

Rate books (which include the poor) are usually with parish records, which means contacting again the CRO, parish church or sometimes libraries, but unfortunately few survive before 1744.

They list householders and/or owners, assessments of property values and rates levied on them. Use them to see when a family first occupied an address, when a street was named perhaps after an ancestor, or when houses were built (again perhaps by an ancestor) because obviously a family must have lived somewhere else previously. Rate books systematically cover streets earlier than do directories, which they complement. Darlington's *Rate Books* gives excellent tips on using these records to best advantage.

Church rates were compulsory from 1601 to 1868. In many localities the parish overseer's records included payment details, but in others a separate book was provided and there may be all kinds of information within it, including what amount to genealogical details. Be on your mettle in using this source, and ever aware of changed street names and house numbers. As with directories, check a few years either side to ensure accuracy.

POLL TAX

This 1377–81 tax (forerunner of income tax) is included only to warn and explain, for it is easily confused with poll books.

The latter are concerned with electors, whereas the tax – sometimes called head tax – was levied on every male over fourteen. Records are at the PRO and those which were printed are at CROs.

HEARTH TAX

Commencing 1668 and repealed 1689, hearth tax demonstrates social and financial position, since 2s was paid for each hearth and a man of means possibly had four. This tax was payable by each householder (not houseowner), so if a man possessed more than one property he was assessed only on any he occupied himself. However, if he used one perhaps as a town residence and another as a country seat then you can expect to find him listed in both places. The records (some printed) are in the PRO and CROs, and are lists headed *in bonis* for the humble and *in terris* for the wealthy, and this itself is helpful.

An untraceable family implies that it was too poor to be charged or perhaps did not have a hearth, the liability falling on those dwellings valued at over 20s a year. Paupers were naturally exempted – a pauper was not necessarily in abject poverty but simply someone requiring parish relief. Normally these individuals would not appear in returns, but in 1664 they were noted along with taxpayers and therefore this is the prime year to seek.

TAX ON BIRTHS, MARRIAGES, BURIALS, WIDOWERS AND BACHELORS

Levied 1694–1706, the few surviving records of this tax are with CROs and guildhalls, occasionally with firms of solicitors, and consequently hard to find. Only childless widowers were liable.

LAND TAX

Of the many taxes inflicted this was about the most crippling, and influenced many a man to vote Tory. Although there were certain land charges from time to time, an effective though fluctuating levy was enforced in 1692 and made permanent in 1797. If you find a man paying land tax it follows, probably from 1745 but perhaps more certainly from 1780, that he had the vote – so the records apply until electoral rolls were introduced in 1832.

Payment was assessed on property values, and the annual records are now normally with the CRO among quarter sessions papers, showing names of owner and occupier (after 1786), a description of the land (after 1826), and assessment. Valuations are as at introduction of this particular tax, and therefore hardly any true guide; but these archives do pin down the more modest men in the role of occupiers.

WINDOW TAX

This tax applied 1747–1851. At its height in 1808 it squeezed from the population 8s for each house with a maximum of six windows, £1 with seven, £1 13s with eight and so on. Hence so many Georgian houses have windows obviously bricked up. The amount of tax paid clearly indicates income and social standing, and in 1825 houses with less than eight windows were exempted in response to popular agitation. Apply to CROs.

There was a window tax in 1695, but then it related only to property assessed above £5, which was then a moderately high valuation.

SERVANT TAX

Certain male servants became taxed through their employers in 1777. They were mainly gamekeepers and household servants, so in practice the gentry were most affected. This tax was extended to include females from 1785, and called for one guinea in each case. Inquire at the CRO.

GAME TAX

Enforced 1784–1807, this was payable by all permitted to kill game and lists include addresses. Chance your arm with the CRO, but during enforcement the law forbade the taking of game by any but squires or their eldest sons.

SHOP TAX

A form of duty enforced in 1785 by William Pitt the Younger, struggling to raise money for consecutive wars, this is useful for tradesmen. Approach the CRO.

HAIRPOWDER TAX

Introduced in 1795, one of the shorter-lived taxes. It greatly contributed to a fashion change, because people naturally begrudged the guinea demanded each year and so ceased to wear wigs. Clergymen were exempt from payment, and in practice those liable were mostly nobility, gentry and their servants. Sometimes records are with clerks of the peace, but mostly their old archives are now with CROs.

CHAPTER TEN

THE LAW

The law perhaps can be divided into landowning, impoverishment and crime.

LANDOWNING

Forms of conveyance are extremely complicated. The oldest was a feoffment, which was a transfer of property ownership designed to circumvent the law concerning medieval feudal duties. From late sixteenth century to 1845 transfer was usually by lease and release, the two always found together. To avoid certain legal procedures, land was leased and immediately thereafter the rights which went with ownership were released. Incidentally written deeds (legally required from 1677) may include mortgage particulars and then often name a bank, which may be also that of the mortgagor or mortgagee, whose account could therefore possibly be traced.

Land laws presented a challenge to be overcome by astute purchasers and vendors. Feet of fines were special types of deeds. An owner would claim he had been robbed of the property, then before court judgement a compromise was reached whereby the one physically in possession could keep the property by financially compensating its legal owner. Thus the case is on the Court of Common Pleas rolls in the PRO, and the copy deed termed a foot of fine. Recoveries – the complexity of which need not trouble you – were deeds to disentail land. Again records are at the PRO for the same court. Both feet of fines and recoveries apply up to 1833.

Since 1925, property title has had to be proved for only fifty years, so deeds may not be all together, the older ones perhaps lying at the CRO or PRO. They help to check boundaries, usually including sketch maps and sometimes furnishings. However, up to 1730 they are normally in Latin,

and those cut through herringbone fashion have been cancelled. Although almost all deeds follow set wording, they
often make extremely difficult reading because of handwriting, legal jargon and language (even the English ones),
and may well require expert advice. However they can be
marvellous sources for compiling whole chunks of pedigrees.

Registration of title commenced in 1704, when registries
began being set up for the then three Yorkshire ridings and
Middlesex (northern London). Nowadays this work is cen-
tralized in the LRO, and gradually the whole of England and
Wales is being covered compulsorily.

You may be fortunate enough to find a firm of solicitors
holding deeds of an interesting property and willing to lend
them or provide photostats. Where property has been inherited, wills feature prominently and copies may well be
with title deeds.

Manorial records are also an obvious place where title
and tenancies are noted. However, they do cover a great
deal more and are found in so many locations (including
private collections) that it is simplest to inquire at the CRO,
where many have been deposited anyway, or to examine the
Historical Manuscripts Commission register. A number are
kept at the PRO. These records extend to at least the nineteenth century and their range within this time limit is almost boundless, since long ago lords of the manor were
virtually local rulers and held courts, in some cases until
1926. They were empowered to grant or refuse permission
for tenants' children to marry, to regulate social behaviour,
grant tenancies, administer church dues, receive rents, im-
pose bylaws, punish petty offences, etc., and frequently kept
very detailed records, so that they throw direct light on the
most humble families. Particularly in the early nineteenth
century, this source is very helpful with farming areas, while
before 1750 they assist greatly with a period for which parish
registers and wills give little help.

Government-decreed enclosure of common land resulted
in very many cases of injustice to the humble to the advantage of the rich, and caused great discontent. Many minor

farmers' sons migrated to towns, because their fathers faced ruin. A man who merely grazed one cow might find himself without rights to do so. Awards (published for some counties) are most often with CROs and the PRO, and cover all but contemporary urban areas 1730–1885, though forms of enclosure date back much further. Frequently they include lists of householders – which do not confuse with houseowners – and maps, though these date from only about 1780 to the early 1900s.

The middle part of England was most affected by official enclosure, elsewhere having been thus regulated long before. Taken as a whole, enclosure was probably the greatest factor – save perhaps the Industrial Revolution – in eliminating peasantry as such in England and Wales.

Tithes were originally one-tenths of the mainly agricultural produce and livestock which were due from owners to the church. Gradually they were commuted into cash payments. When enclosure was introduced payment became either cash or land, the former being related to corn prices and known as corn rent; and tithe maps were attached to enclosure awards, listing owners, occupiers, descriptions and uses of property. Apart from being at CROs, maps and apportionments are also at the PRO up to 1936. In addition, the Tithe Redemption Office should have all maps dated 1836, the office's seal being the only guarantee of true accuracy regarding tithe maps. They relate to urban as well as rural areas and are effectively superseded by Ordnance Survey maps.

Copyhold land has a manorial roll copy as title, and quit rent is usually payment by a freeholder or copyholder in lieu of service to the Crown or whoever the owner was. Peppercorn rent is merely symbolic payment. Messuage means a dwelling-house with adjoining buildings, curtilage (yard) and perhaps land; an oxgang is as much land as an ox can plough annually, i.e. 13–20 acres; a toft is ground on which a house stands, but a croft is pasture or tillage land adjoining it.

IMPOVERISHMENT

Impoverishment has been treated almost as a crime until comparatively recently, though many sincere individuals tried to alleviate true distress. This is abundantly evident in the many charities still existing for orphaned, infirm, aged and mentally ill, with their institutions perhaps still housing their own old records.

In 1662 the law of settlement and removal was introduced and workhouses were constituted in 1722, which latter – although having fearful and shameful connotations for the old and unemployed – had perhaps the best intentions in providing theoretically at least shelter, education, medicinal aid and work for the able.

Overseers of the poor existed from medieval times, records (usually with CROs) including notes on paupers' pensions from about 1600. They were responsible until 1834 under the Poor Relief Act 1662 for removing from their parishes individuals who threatened to become rates burdens. Thus the humble were supposed to obtain settlement certificates from their home parishes if they wished to travel, and were returnable to that parish if necessary. From 1691 people could obtain settlement through apprenticeship, regular employment, rates payment and other means, but it was not automatic for parishes to accept responsibility for them merely by virtue of birth. Removal orders often give extensive genealogical information. Many relate to pregnant women because overseers had no wish to have yet another child to worry about. After 1834 poor families were sent to workhouses.

Others seeking parish relief were travellers who were licensed as genuine, including seamen, soldiers, etc., and these were documented too.

Overseers of the poor were succeeded by boards of guardians in 1834, who continued their work until 1929 and whose records should be with CROs, also.

Impoverishment can apply even to a formerly wealthy family through recklessness, carelessness or sheer bad luck. Cases were published in *Perry's Bankrupt & Insolvent Gazette*, as well as newspapers, and victims were confined in debtors' prisons. Records, which are sometimes difficult to trace, should be with quarter sessions papers but have often been lost or mislaid in council or legal offices – not nearly enough being safeguarded in CROs.

CRIME

Criminal and civil offences have long been the province of magistrates (later also styled justices of the peace). These officials met in quarter sessions with juries and individually tried minor cases in petty sessions, but major trials were held by judges at assizes. Once manorial courts tried local offenders, as also did church courts, and for all three types of archive (earliest about 1550) inquire at CROs. The PRO also holds records in Home Office archives. The more lurid the crime, the more likely it was reported in a newspaper, which may also list forthcoming trials.

Cases are myriad – vagrancy, witchcraft, stealing, slander, murder, adultery, bigamy, assault, rioting, poaching, trespassing, etc. Punishments range from fines and property confiscation to ducking, flogging, pillorying, imprisonment, the stocks, hanging, and transportation for any period up to life. Transportation features 1787–1870 under seafaring records in the PRO, where also are details of most convicts from at least 1782. With luck you will find ages to complement crime and punishment details.

Suicide was an offence until recently, incorporated in coroners' records, again often newspaper-reported and again theoretically in CROs. Coroners were concerned, too, with deaths in prison by natural causes, capital punishment and in any sudden or suspect circumstances. City of London records are at Guildhall from 1788, but sometimes in peculiar shorthand.

If you trace an ancestor to prison curb your alarm! Eighteenth-century horse- and sheep-stealing were capital crimes, as was stealing of most kinds and coining. Conversely murderers' treatment might be lenient in an age when duels were fought and cutting a nose could risk death. Naturally the law is geared to the times and has always been highly complex, and many acquittals have been surprising.

CROs are usually custodians of 'Tyburn tickets', which were certificates exempting from parish duties apprehenders of capitally punished criminals. They are dated 1699–1827.

CHAPTER ELEVEN.

SOCIAL HISTORY

Courtesy titles were used formerly with great correctness. Everyone 'knew their place' and kept within rigid classes. Never omit 'Mr' (originally 'Master') in copying records, because it implies community standing and respect, was unfailingly used in conversation by a man's inferiors, and was inherited automatically by his son unless that son had fallen socially. More impressive was 'Gentleman'. This was attached to the professions and men of independent means, sometimes after retirement.

Until around 1800 'clerk' was used only in describing clergymen. 'Esquire' implied a Crown commission – civil, naval or military – with 'yeoman' ranking next to it. Up to the sixteenth century freehold landholders owing service to king or abbey were called 'sokemen'. 'Dame' originally was a knight's wife and not, as now, his counterpart and is not connected with dames' schools. 'Mistress' has become 'Mrs' but until early eighteenth century meant a refined spinster.

The social structure was closely allied to the vote through landowning. Land-tax assessment (Chapter Nine) was a necessary qualification from 1780, though theoretically from 1745, for which CROs may have poll books. Up to 1832 only those owning freehold worth at least 40s a year were enfranchised, then gradually parliamentary reforms extended voting to most urban, though not rural, working men by 1867. In 1918 women over 30 were enfranchised, in 1928 everyone over 21 and in 1970 all over 18. From 1842 county sheriffs' poll books (not to be confused with poll tax) list all electors and occupations, for which again ask your CRO.

Electoral rolls or voters' registers at CROs provide research pointers as well as addresses, which may not be residences. Those earlier than 1872 show a man's political persuasion, there being no secret ballot and there may have been many reasons why his vote was swayed. Jurors are noted on electoral rolls also, which is a broad guide to property ownership.

Education features doubly in your research: educational records and subsequent application of learning. The rich were tutored at home originally, but the poor went unlettered for centuries. By 1500, when Winchester and Eton were no longer young, there were many private, monastic, grammar and even public schools. They catered for the upper and middle classes before entry into Oxford or Cambridge Universities at the progressively later age of 14–18, practised strict discipline, and were heavily biased in favour of Latin, necessary for most careers from that of ordinary scribe upwards. By the 1600s grammar schools had become English education's backbone. Many enjoyed excellent reputations and I have a beautifully written 1835 exercise book belonging to a Northallerton boy, on fairly advanced mathematics.

Initial attempts were made with eighteenth-century dames' schools and charity schools to include poor children, presaging Victorian reforms, though this coincided with the decline of many grammar schools. About 1790, Dissenters' academies were instituted by Methodists and others to bolster other private education. Not much more than a basic curriculum was involved there or at the Church-administered national establishments, although these last did make definite efforts to bring the working class a literacy greatly weighted in favour of religion and an awareness of 'place'. Early nineteenth-century secondary education was still the upper class prerogative.

The year 1870 saw the founding of government-controlled primary Board Schools, while in 1902 responsibility was vested in county schools for both primary and secondary education.

Compulsory education of sorts began in 1833 but was not really effective until the Elementary Education Act 1870 (and then only for children under twelve), supplemented by the Free Education Act 1891. Consideration of education must allow for children's working hours, as they still worked even when two hours' daily schooling became law.

Records are variously preserved. Schools having long been spokes revolving round the Church hub, you may find existing records with incumbents (Established and other) as well as with schools themselves or at CROs. Mostly they are Victorian but a few reach back to the sixteenth century – mainly for grammar schools and sometimes compiled by ardent masters, such as Lawson's *A Town Grammar School through Six Centuries* for Hull. There may be lists of pupils, occasionally mentioning fathers. Masters may appear in registers of bishops, who once licensed them. Naturally public schools generally have good archives. Universities (see Chapter Eight) admitted women from 1860, and people from all religions soon afterwards. All these documents may provide you with genealogical material.

Mechanics' institutes were born in 1823 with the Industrial Revolution. Ask your CRO about these also.

Orphans and foundlings were wretched little souls, frequently just left to die until the first Foundling Hospital was set up in London in 1745. Registers are with the PRO. In 1866 Dr Barnardo opened his first orphanage, since when hundreds of thousands of children have been recorded by his homes including numerous photographs.

Not all orphans have been homeless, of course. Many of all social classes have been wards of court since Norman days, and from 1540 their archives are in the PRO among Chancery papers. At some time every family has been thus concerned. Helpfully, funds in Chancery are published in the *London Gazette*.

Many metropolitan and provincial banks sprang up from the seventeenth century, though a great number failed, particularly through issuing their own banknotes and thus ruining their clients. The Post Office Savings Bank dates from 1861, trustee savings banks throughout Britain from 1827 and the Bank of England from 1694. There have been almost countless mergers, but it is relatively simple to trace these and to discover what existed at a given time from town directories and local histories, whereafter particulars of individual accounts are sometimes found. Apply direct to the bank.

Family documents may still be held privately or entrusted to CROs, but ask your library about those printed or check with the Historical Manuscripts Commission. They embrace the whole social stratum, as servants or tenants were usually included. If there is a coat-of-arms or official crest it should be registered with the College of Arms, but many Victorians simply assumed crests, which were uncommon before about 1550. Heraldry is a separate subject, but each facet has significance and large colour-illustrated volumes in libraries depict all armorial bearings, past and present.

The heralds toured England 1530–1687 to establish every genuine right to arms by direct male descent over minimally three generations, so if your progress is extensive enough delve into heralds' visitations at the BL for nobility and gentry or see if your library can provide a printed copy. Tracing back to 1700 or so probably means your forebears had at least some connection with gentry. Visitations are not infallible owing to errors of memory, so that descent may not have been strictly father to son and pedigrees may be incomplete. Check with inquisitions post mortem. Heraldry is fraught with risk for the uninitiated, but assistance is available from the Heraldry Society.

Document seals, perhaps impressed from rings, may be indicative of status. Generally merchants and landed gentry adopted birds, animals, trees or flowers, knights favouring horses. However, many are simply plain lozenges – diamond shapes preferred by ladies, who still remain ineligible to use coats-of-arms except by incorporating their fathers' with their husbands'.

Religious restrictions involving civic rights and worship were widespread until late nineteenth century, causing CROs particularly to hold many extra documents. Sessions rolls note Dissenters' meeting houses, with Papists and Nonconformists who failed to attend Established Church services. Also in these rolls are Sacrament certificates and declarations denying Transubstantiation, required under the Test Act 1673 which obliged all civil officials and army or navy officers to receive the Sacrament according to Church of England rites. These are supplemented by oaths of allegiance (1722 and later) obligatory in England on everyone over eighteen, and by lists of Catholic landholdings from 1715.

Naturally, epidemics all too often accompanied bad sanitation – some national, others needing local research. The best known is the 1665 Great Plague, so-called because it was merely the worst of many following the Black Death. The seventeenth-century nationwide infant mortality rate was nearly 30 per cent, in the next century London's was as high as 75 per cent, which fell to about 30 per cent in the next fifty years. Death at any age was thus commonplace – more so because of prevalent smallpox, cholera and such than because of highwaymen on bad roads terrorizing the riding rich if not the walking poor.

Much drunkenness and brawling occurred despite or because of usually low wages coupled with rising population, and Londoners' surroundings were foul-smelling from littered streets flanked by often stagnant ditches. Provincial towns were hardly better: Newcastle was noted for industrial smoke, though resorts like Bath and York also lent grace if only for the rich to enjoy their many pleasures. Water supplies had begun improving by 1810 along with the introduction of sewers and drains, but efforts were still generally pathetic by 1840. People were slow to cease tipping excrement and garbage into the streets. Even London was without general sewers until 1865 – a bare hundred years ago! However, vaccination was introduced around 1800 and later made compulsory, which was a massive step forward in controlling smallpox.

CROs hold many papers dealing with all this and with lunacy. Overseers and later boards of guardians registered parish-burden lunatics after 1815 – apart from earlier mental cases annotated in various documents – and after 1832 private asylums made obligatory reports.

London north of the Thames was formerly embraced by the erstwhile county of Middlesex and is exceedingly well documented, particularly by the Middlesex Archaeological Society. This is noteworthy especially because eighteenth-century French Huguenot Protestant refugees settled in numbers around Spitalfields and Shoreditch. Some became private tutors, but most were connected with silk and lace trades.

CHAPTER TWELVE

MOBILITY

Travel was formerly no easy undertaking. A moneyed man might have a horse, maybe a coach, but even eighteenth-century roads were terrible. The humbler relied on their feet or in dire need a cart. Though introduced in 1658, stage-coaches reached their zenith 1820–40, after which most ceased to operate. Their and carters' services appear in town directories.

From 1663, eventually ending in 1895, tolls and turnpikes financed road improvements invariably undertaken by turn-pike trusts, and CROs usually have documents regarding shareholders. This apart, the actual highway routes naturally point in which direction a family may have moved (perhaps village to town) and it is amazing how much population mobility existed.

Railways emerged properly from 1830, creating far greater travel opportunities. British Transport Historical Records Office can advise when the various companies were formed, lines established and accidents occurred, as well as giving information regarding shareholders and staff. Personnel are also recorded by trade unions.

EMIGRANTS

Tracing forebears who settled abroad can be extremely lengthy, exhausting, costly, difficult and finally unrewarding. Not that documentation is wanting, but that searching requires much prior knowledge. Vestry minutes can be very useful.

The PRO can help with visitors and settlers in all British Dominions and Colonies and in foreign territories, sometimes back to 1540. Its American records include the Pilgrim Fathers, West Indian plantations, Loyalists' compensation, transported convicts 1719–44 (some indexed) and others. (USA archives relating to immigrants are with the General Services Administration, National Archives & Records Service).

You may find land grants, correspondence, pensions, official appointments, sea passengers from 1890, monetary payments, lawsuits, shareholdings, etc. Those convicts transported to Australasia are divided into New South Wales and Tasmania, commonly with details of genealogy and offences and with special census returns incorporating families which had been born to them overseas or had followed the convicted, allowing for heavy loss of life on passage.

Some military pensioners were among emigrants to Australia and New Zealand 1846–51. These and general migrants 1773–6 to various places, including America, are all chronicled in the PRO, too, some providing choice titbits such as motives. A further register series there deals with passports 1795–1898.

IMMIGRANTS

Britain has been a recognized goal of immigrants since about 1200, often resulting from trade considerations or religious persecution. Naturally not all newcomers were refugees. The Irish and Jews came in thousands in the eighteenth century, the first being slum-dwelling cheap labour and the other moneylenders and great bankers.

Among the most important are Huguenots, who entered in great numbers periodically from about 1523 and settled mainly in London but also in centres like Norwich, Exeter and Plymouth. Some expanded English horticulture, and the Englishman's love of gardening is attributed mainly to Dutch Huguenots. The Huguenot Society of London publications include various indexed returns of aliens 1523–61, and other nationalities particularly covered by them are French and Walloon (French-speaking Belgian).

The PRO issues a leaflet specifically outlining its wealth of immigrant detail. Much is similar to that mentioned above, plus foreign London merchants' transactions (thirteenth–

seventeenth centuries), naturalizations (about 1400–1924), various registers of French, Dutch, German and Swiss refugees (1567–1857), Crown pensions (1557–1728), etc. Incorporated will be found trades, origins, British residences, signatures, ship (but not aircraft) passengers, and ages. Not all the French, of course, were Huguenots: many fled the Revolution. Some of the Dutch were merely en route to America.

Other repositories of foreigners' records are the British, Bodleian, Cambridge University and Lambeth Palace libraries, House of Lords Record Office, London's Guildhall and the Society of Genealogists. Naturalizations are printed in the *London Gazette*.

GENERAL ADDRESSES

Bodleian Library, Oxford.

Borthwick Institute of Historical Research, St Anthony's Hall, York.

British Library, Store Street, London WC1; Reading & Map Rooms at British Museum, Great Russell Street, London WC1.

British Museum, Great Russell Street, London WC1.

British Transport Historical Records Office, *see* PRO, Kew.

Cambridge University Library, Cambridge.

Catholic Record Society, 48 Lowndes Square, London SW1.

Church Commissioners, 1 Millbank, Westminster, London SW1.

College of Arms, Queen Victoria Street, London EC4.

Corporation of London Record Office, Guildhall, London EC2.

Faculty Office, The Sanctuary, Westminster, London SW1.

Federation of Family History Societies, 19 Harboro Road, Sale, Greater Manchester.

Foreign & Commonwealth Office, 197 Blackfriars Road, London SE1.

General Register Office: *Eire*: Custom House, Dublin; *England and Wales*: General certificates – St Catherine's House, Kingsway, London WC2; Divorce – Somerset House, Strand, London WC2; *Northern Ireland*: Fermanagh House, Belfast; *Scotland*: New Register House, Edinburgh.

Guildhall, Basinghall Street, London EC2.

Guildhall Library, Aldermanbury, London EC2.

Heralds' College, Queen Victoria Street, London EC4.

Heraldry Society, 28 Museum Street, London WC1.

Historical Manuscripts Commission, Quality House, Quality Court, Chancery Lane, London WC2.

House of Lords Record Office, Westminster, London SW1.

Huguenot Society of London, 1 Pall Mall East, London SW1.

Imperial War Museum, Lambeth Road, London SE1.

Institute of Heraldic & Genealogical Studies, Northgate, Canterbury, Kent.

Irish Genealogical Research Society, c/o The Irish Club, 82 Eaton Square, London SW1.

Jewish Historical Society of England, Mocatta Library, University College, London WC1.

Lambeth Palace Library, Lambeth Palace, London SE1.

Land Registry Office, Portugal Street, London WC2.

Law Society, 113 Chancery Lane, London WC2.

Law Society of Scotland, Drumsheugh Gardens, Edinburgh.

Lloyd's Register of Shipping, Fenchurch Street, London EC3.

Methodists' Archives & Research Centre, Epworth House, City Road, London EC1.

Middlesex Archaeological Society, Bishopsgate Institute, Bishopsgate, London EC2.

Military Historical Society, Duke of York's Headquarters, Chelsea, London SW3.

Ministry of Defence ARS (RAF), Adastral House, Theobalds Road, London WC1.

Museum of London, Aldersgate Street, London EC1.

National Army Museum, Royal Hospital Road, Chelsea, London SW3.

National Library of Ireland, Kildare Street, Dublin.

National Library of Scotland, George IV Bridge, Edinburgh.

National Library of Wales, Aberystwyth, Dyfed.

National Maritime Museum, Greenwich, London SE10.

National Museum of Antiquities of Scotland, Queen Street, Edinburgh.

National Museum of Wales, Cardiff.

Navy Records Society, Royal Naval College, Greenwich, London SE10.

Newspaper Library, Colindale Avenue, Colindale, London NW9.

Principal Probate Registry, Somerset House, Strand, London WC2.

Public Record Office, Four Courts & Record Tower, The Castle, Dublin.

Public Record Office, Ruskin Avenue, Kew, Greater London (headquarters) and Chancery Lane, London WC2.

Public Record Office of Northern Ireland, Balmoral Avenue, Belfast.

Raymond Mander & Joe Mitchenson Theatre Collection, 5 Venner Road, Sydenham, London SE26.

Registrar General, Government House, Douglas, Isle of Man.

Royal Air Force Association, 43 Grove Park Road, London W4.

Royal Humane Society, Watergate House, York Buildings, Adelphi, London WC2.

Royal Institution of Cornwall, River Street, Truro, Cornwall.

Royal Scottish Museum, Chambers Street, Edinburgh.

Scottish Genealogical Society, 21 Howard Place, Edinburgh.

Scottish Record Office, PO Box 36, General Register House, Princes Street, Edinburgh.

Society for Army Historical Research, c/o The Library, Old War Office Building, Whitehall, London SW1.

Society of Friends, Friends House, Euston Road, London NW1.

Society of Genealogists, 37 Harrington Gardens, Kensington, London SW7.

Tithe Redemption Office, Barrington Road, Worthing, Sussex.

Ulster-Scot Historical Society, Law Courts Building, Chichester Street, Belfast.

United Grand Lodge of England, Freemasons Hall, Great Queen Street, London WC2.

Welsh Folk Museum, St Fagans, Cardiff.

Dr Williams's Library, Gordon Square, London WC1.

OVERSEAS ADDRESSES

Australia Society of Australian Genealogists, Heritage House, 413 Riley Street, Surry Hills, NSW 2010.

Austria Staatsarchiv, Landstrasse Hauptstrasse 140, Vienna.

Belgium L'Archiviste Générale, 78 Galerie Ravenstein, Brussels.

Canada Public Archives of Canada, 330 Sussex Drive, Ottawa, Ontario.

Channel Islands excluding Jersey Registrar General's Office, Greffe, Guernsey.

France Conservateur aux Archives Nationales, 60 Rue des Frances-Bourgeois, Paris IIIe.

Germany Verein für Heraldik, Genealogie und verwandte Wissenschaften, Westfälischestrasse 38, Berlin-Halensee.

Holland Koninklijk Nederlandsch Genootschap voor Geslacht en Wapenkunde, Bleijenburg 5, The Hague.

Indian Continent Foreign & Commonwealth Office, 197 Blackfriars Road, London SE1.

Italy Istituto Centrale di Statistica, Via Cesare Balbo 16, Rome.

Jersey Superintendent Registrar, States Building, St Helier.

New Zealand New Zealand Society of Genealogists, 70 Allendale Road, Mount Albert, Auckland.

Portugal Instituto Portugues de Heraldica, Largo do Carmo, Lisbon.

South Africa Genealogical Society of South Africa, 40 Haylett Street Strand, Capetown.

Spain Cuerpo de Cronistas Reyes de Armas, Ministerio de Justicia, Calle de San Bernardo 45, Madrid 8.

Switzerland Schweizerische Heraldische Gesellschaft, Château de Marnex, 1299 Commugny.

USA General Services Administration, National Archives & Record Services, Washington 25, D.C.

COUNTY RECORD OFFICES

Avon   South: CRO, Obridge Road, Taunton, Somerset; North: CRO, Shire Hall, Gloucester; Bristol: Archives Office, Council House, Bristol, Avon.

Bedfordshire: CRO, County Hall, Bedford.

Berkshire: CRO, Shire Hall, Reading, Berkshire.

Buckinghamshire: CRO, County Offices, Aylesbury, Buckinghamshire.

Cambridgeshire: Old county & Isle of Ely: CRO, Shire Hall, Cambridge.

  Huntingdonshire: RO, Huntingdon, Cambridgeshire.

  Wisbech: Wisbech & Fenland Museum, Museum Square, Wisbech, Cambridgeshire.

  Peterborough: CRO, Delapré Abbey, London Road, Northampton.

Cheshire: CRO, The Castle, Chester.

  Old Lancashire: Public Library, Warrington, Cheshire.

  Chester: City RO, Town Hall, Chester.

Cleveland: CRO, Central Library, Middlesbrough, Cleveland.

  Old Yorkshire: CRO, County Hall, Northallerton, North Yorkshire.

  Old County Durham: CRO, County Hall, Durham.

Cornwall: CRO, County Hall, Truro, Cornwall.

  Truro: Royal Institution of Cornwall, River Street, Truro, Cornwall.

Cumbria: CRO, The Castle, Carlisle, Cumbria.

  Westmorland, old Yorkshire & Furness: County Offices, Kendal, Cumbria.

Derbyshire: CRO, County Offices, Matlock, Derbyshire.

  Derby: Public Library, Wardwick, Derbyshire.

Devon: CRO, Concord House, South Street, Exeter, Devon.

  Exeter: City RO, Central Library, Exeter, Devon.

  Plymouth: Central Library, Tavistock Road, Plymouth, Devon.

Dorset: CRO, County Hall, Dorchester, Dorset.

Durham: CRO, County Hall, Durham.
Durham City: Department of Palaeography & Diplomatic, University of Durham, Durham.
Darlington: Public Library, Darlington, Durham.
East Sussex: CRO, Pelham House, St Andrew's Lane, Lewes, East Sussex.
Essex: CRO, County Hall, Chelmsford, Essex.
Southend: Central Library, Southend-on-Sea, Essex.
Gloucestershire: CRO, Shire Hall, Gloucester.
Gloucester: Central Library, Brunswick Road, Gloucester.
Greater London: CRO, County Hall, Kingston-upon-Thames, Greater London.
RO, County Hall, London SE1.
Middlesex: CRO, 1 Queen Anne's Gate Buildings, Dartmouth Street, London SW1.
City: Corporation of London Record Office, Guildhall, London EC2.
Greater Manchester: CRO, Sessions House, Lancaster Road, Preston, Lancashire.
Stockport: Central Library, Stockport, Greater Manchester.
Salford: Central Library, Swinton, Salford, Greater Manchester.
Wigan: Public Library, Wigan, Greater Manchester.
Manchester: Central Library, Manchester.
Bolton: Central Library, Bolton, Greater Manchester.
Hampshire: CRO, 20 Southgate Street, Winchester, Hampshire.
Portsmouth: RO, Guildhall, Portsmouth, Hampshire.
Southampton: RO, Civic Centre, Southampton, Hampshire.
Winchester: City RO, Guildhall, Winchester, Hampshire.
Hereford & Worcester: CRO, Shirehall, Foregate Street, Worcester.
Herefordshire: RO, The Old Barracks, Harold Street, Hereford.
Worcestershire: RO, St Helen's, Fish Street, Worcester.
Hertfordshire: CRO, County Hall, Hertford.
Humberside: CRO, County Hall, Beverley, Humberside.
Lincolnshire: Archives Office, The Castle, Lincoln.
Hull: City RO, Guildhall, Kingston-upon-Hull, Humberside.
Kent: Archives Office, County Hall, Maidstone, Kent.
Canterbury: Cathedral Library, Canterbury, Kent.
Lancashire: CRO, Sessions House, Lancaster Road, Preston, Lancashire.
Bowland: County Hall, Wakefield, West Yorkshire.
Leicestershire: CRO, New Walk, Leicester.
Lincolnshire: Archives Office, The Castle, Lincoln.

Man, Isle of: General Registry, Douglas, Isle of Man.

Merseyside: CRO, Sessions House, Lancaster Road, Preston, Lancashire.

   Liverpool: RO, Brown Library, Liverpool, Merseyside.

   Wirral: Central Library, Birkenhead, Merseyside.

Norfolk: RO, Central Library, Norwich, Norfolk.

North Yorkshire: CRO, County Hall, Northallerton, North Yorkshire.

   York: County Library, Museum Street, York, North Yorkshire.

   Old Yorkshire: Archives Department, Sheepscar Library, Chapeltown Road, Leeds, West Yorkshire.

Northamptonshire: CRO, Delapré Abbey, London Road, Northampton.

Northumberland: CRO, Melton Park, North Gosforth, Newcastle-upon-Tyne, Tyne & Wear.

Nottinghamshire: CRO, County House, High Pavement, Nottingham.

   Nottingham: City RO, Guildhall, Nottingham.

Oxfordshire: CRO, County Hall, New Road, Oxford.

   Bodleian Library, Oxford.

   Oxford City: Central Library, Westgate, Oxford.

Salop: CRO, Shirehall, Abbey Foregate, Shrewsbury, Salop.

   Shrewsbury: Town Library, Shrewsbury, Salop.

Somerset: CRO, Obridge Road, Taunton, Somerset.

South Yorkshire: CRO, City Library, Sheffield, South Yorkshire.

Staffordshire: RO, County Buildings, Eastgate Street, Stafford.

   RO, Public Library, Bird Street, Lichfield, Staffordshire.

Suffolk: East Suffolk: CRO, County Hall, Ipswich, Suffolk.

   West Suffolk: CRO, School Hall Street, Bury St Edmunds, Suffolk.

Surrey: CRO, County Hall, Kingston-upon-Thames, Greater London.

Tyne & Wear: CRO, 109 Pilgrim Street, Newcastle-upon-Tyne, Tyne & Wear.

Warwickshire: CRO, Priory Park, Cape Road, Warwick.

   Stratford: Shakespeare's Birthplace Trust Library, Henley Street, Stratford-on-Avon, Warwickshire.

   Warwick: University Library, Warwick.

West Midlands: Warwickshire: CRO, Priory Park, Cape Road, Warwick.

   Staffordshire: RO, Public Library, Bird Street, Lichfield, Staffordshire.

Birmingham: Central Reference Library, Birmingham, West Midlands.

Also University Library, Birmingham, West Midlands.

Coventry: City RO, 9 Hay Lane, Coventry, West Midlands.

West Sussex: CRO, John Edes House, West Street, Chichester, West Sussex.

Old East Sussex: CRO, Pelham House, Lewes, East Sussex.

West Yorkshire: CRO, County Hall, Wakefield, West Yorkshire.

Archives Department, Sheepscar Library, Chapeltown Road, Leeds, West Yorkshire.

Wight, Isle of: CRO, 26 Hillside, Newport, Isle of Wight.

Wiltshire: CRO, County Hall, Trowbridge, Wiltshire.

WALES

Clwyd: CRO, The Old Rectory, Hawarden, Deeside, Clwyd.

Denbighshire: RO, 46 Clwyd Street, Ruthin, Clwyd.

Dyfed: Carmarthenshire: CRO, County Hall, Carmarthen, Dyfed.

Pembrokeshire: RO, The Castle, Haverfordwest, Dyfed.

Cardiganshire: RO, Marine Terrace, Aberystwyth, Dyfed.

Tenby Museum, Tenby, Dyfed.

Gwent: CRO, County Hall, Cwmbran, Gwent.

Gwynedd: Anglesey: Area RO, County Hall, Llangefni, Ynys Môn, Gwynedd.

Merionethshire: Area RO, Y Lawnt, Dolgellau, Gwynedd.

Denbighshire: see Clwyd.

Caernarfonshire: Area RO, Caernarfon, Gwynedd.

Mid Glamorgan: CRO, County Hall, Cardiff, South Glamorgan.

Powys: National Library of Wales, Aberystwyth, Dyfed.

South Glamorgan: CRO, County Hall, Cardiff, South Glamorgan.

West Glamorgan: CRO, County Hall, Cardiff, South Glamorgan.

BIBLIOGRAPHY

Andrews, John. *Ireland in Maps* (1961)

Burke's Colonial Gentry

Burke's Commoners

Burke's Dormant & Extinct Peerages

Burke's Family Index (1976)

Burke's General Armory (see page 113)

Burke's Landed Gentry

Burke's Peerage, Baronetage & Knightage

Burns, Nancie. *Family Tree* (1962) – simplicity, readability and sound guidelines but now unfortunately outdated for locations.

Calthrop, D. C. *English Costume*, Vols 1–4 (1906) – early English to Georgian

Camp, A. J. *An Index to the Wills Proved in the Prerogative Court of Canterbury 1750–1800* (1976–)

Camp, A. J. *Wills & Their Whereabouts* (1963 privately revised 1974)

Carr, A. D. *Deeds of Title* (Historical Association Short Guides to Records No. 12)

Clare, W. *A Simple Guide to Irish Genealogy* (1967)

Cole & Postgate. *The Common People* (1946)

Consulting Engineers' Who's Who

Crockford's Clerical Directory

Darlington, Ida. *Rate Books* (Historical Association Short Guides to Records No. 1)

Debrett's Peerage, Baronetage, Knightage & Companionage

Dictionary of National Biography

Diplomatic Service List

Directory of Directors

Emmison, F. G. *Archives & Local History* (1966)

Emmison, F. G. & Gray, Irvine. *County Records* (1973)

Firth, Sir Charles & Davies, Godfrey. *The Regimental History of Cromwell's Army* (1940)

Foster, Joseph. *Alumni Oxonienses*, Vols 1–4 (1891)

Galsworthy, John. *The Forsyte Saga* (1905–33)

Gardner, D. E., Harland, D. & Smith, Frank. *Genealogical Atlas of England and Wales* (1968)

Genealogists, Society of. *Catalogue of Parish Register Copies*, Part 1 Society of Genealogists Collection, Part 2 Other than Society of Genealogists Collection (Chichester 1970–1)

Genealogists, Society of. *Guide to Handwriting*

Gibson, J. S. W. *Wills & Where to Find Them* (1974)

Goss, C. W. F. *The London Directories* (1932)

Hamilton-Edwards, Gerald. *In Search of Ancestry* (Chichester 1974)

Hamilton-Edwards, Gerald. *In Search of Scottish Ancestry* (Chichester 1972)

Harben, Henry A. *Dictionary of London* (1918), London plans sixteenth–eighteenth centuries, old churches, alleys and streets

Harley, J. B. & Phillips, C. W. *Historian's Guide to Ordnance Survey Maps* (1964)

Hector, L. C. *The Handwriting of English Documents* (1966)

HM Stationery Office. *Guide to the Contents of the Public Record Office*, Vols 1–3 (1963 and 1969)

Humphery-Smith, Cecil R. *General Armory Two: Alfred Morant's Additions & Corrections to Burke's General Armory* (1973) (see page 113)

Iredale, David. *Enjoying Archives* (Newton Abbot 1973)

Jewish Historical Society of England. *Anglo-Jewish Notabilities* (1949)

Lawson, John. *A Town Grammar School through Six Centuries* (Kingston-upon-Hull 1963)

Lewis, Samuel. *Topographical Dictionary of England* (1831–3)

Marshall, G. W. *The Genealogists' Guide* (1973)

Martin, C. T. *Record Interpreter* (1949) – Latin abbreviations, glossary of Latin words in documents, Latin equivalents of English names

Massey, R. S. *List of Parishes in Boyd's Marriage Index* (Chichester 1974)

Mayhew, Henry. *London Labour & the London Poor* (1864)

Medical Register

National Index of Parish Registers (Chichester 1966–)

Newspaper Press Directory

Norton, Jane E. *Guide to National & Provincial Directories of England & Wales, excluding London, published before 1856* (1950)

Page, W. *Denisations & Naturalisations of Aliens in England 1509–1603* (1893)

Papworth, J. W. *Ordinary of British Armorials* (1961)

Peacock, Edward. *The Army List of Roundheads & Cavaliers* (1865)

Public Record Office. *Records of the Colonial & Dominions Offices* (1964)

Reaney, P. H. *Dictionary of British Surnames* (1961)

Richardson, John. *The Local Historian's Encyclopedia* (New Barnet 1974)

Royal Institute of British Architects' Directory

Sharpe France, R. *Wills* (Historical Association Short Guides to Records No. 10)

Shaw, W. A. *Letters of Denisation & Acts of Naturalisation for Aliens in England 1603–1800* (Lymington 1911–23) – Huguenot Vols 18, 27, 35

Swinson, Arthur. *A Register of the Regiments & Corps of the British Army* (1972)

Tate, W. E. *The Parish Chest* (1969)

Thomson, T. R. *A Catalogue of British Family Histories* (1976)

The Times Handlist of English & Welsh Newspapers 1620–1920 (1920)

Trevelyan, G. M. *English Social History*, Vols 1–4 (1942)

Venn, J. *Alumni Cantabrigienses* (1922)

Victoria County History

Walpole, Sir Hugh. *Herries Chronicle* (1930–3)

West, J. *Village Records* (1962)

Whitaker's Almanack

Who Was Who

Who's Who

Withycombe, E. G. *Oxford Dictionary of English Christian Names* (1953) – origins and dates, some special connotations

Wright, A. *Court Hand Restored* (1818)

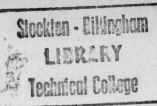

INDEX

A selection of Mayflower War Books

Fiction

THE STORIES OF FLYING OFFICER X	H. E. Bates	50p	☐
SOLDIER FROM THE SEA	Alexander Fullerton	50p	☐
A WREN CALLED SMITH	Alexander Fullerton	40p	☐
THE WAITING GAME	Alexander Fullerton	35p	☐
SURFACE!	Alexander Fullerton	35p	☐
HANGING ON	Dean R. Koontz	60p	☐
'H.M.S. MARLBOROUGH WILL ENTER HARBOUR'	Nicholas Monsarrat	60p	☐
THREE CORVETTES	Nicholas Monsarrat	40p	☐
THE KILLERS: THE WINSTON CHURCHILL MURDER	Klaus Netzen	35p	☐
THE KILLERS: NIGHT AND FOG	Klaus Netzen	40p	☐
THE KILLERS: THE FATAL FRIENDS	Klaus Netzen	40p	☐
THE KILLERS: PEARL OF BLOOD	Klaus Netzen	40p	☐
THE KILLERS: DEATH VILLAGE	Klaus Netzen	40p	☐
THE KILLERS: THE SILENT ENEMY	Klaus Netzen	50p	☐
MOSCOW	Theodor Plievier	60p	☐
STALINGRAD	Theodor Plievier	60p	☐
BERLIN	Theodor Plievier	75p	☐
ALL QUIET ON THE WESTERN FRONT	Erich Maria Remarque	50p	☐
WINGED VICTORY	V. M. Yeates	75p	☐

Non-Fiction

AS FAR AS MY FEET WILL CARRY ME	J. M. Bauer	50p	☐
BOMBER PILOT	Leonard Cheshire	50p	☐
HUNTING THE BISMARCK	C. S. Forester	25p	☐
LONELY WARRIOR	Jean Offenberg	40p	☐
SINK THE TIRPITZ!	Leonce Peillard	75p	☐
POPSKI'S PRIVATE ARMY	Vladimir Peniakoff	75p	☐

Mayflower Handbooks for your information